Quantum Shift
Into
Greatness

Arthur James Tassinello

Quantum Shift Into Greatness

Cover design and artwork by Alan Tomasetti

Layout by Matthew Wayne Selznick mattselznick.com

ISBN-10: 1-4486-4532-8

ISBN-13/EAN-13: 978-1-4486-4532-9

Acknowledgments

Without the love, support, efforts and kindness of so many people throughout my life this book would not have come into existence. Through these wonderful people, my education and experiences I have garnered valuable information and knowledge to improve my life and form greater, better relationships, find happiness and success.

To my mom and dad who raised me with love and kindness, and who are always with me in spirit, thank you for your lessons. I love and miss so very much.

To my son Anthony and my daughter Ali, who decided to enter this world in my care, thank you for the rewarding and beautiful experience of being a parent. The love we share is unparalleled from any other relationship and I thank you for your care and support.

To my beautiful, loving sister Michele, thank you for your love, support and encouragement and for our weekly, almost daily talks.

To Anne, thank you for helping raise our beautiful daughter and whose relationship allowed me to see the world from a new perspective and for your encouragement and belief in me.

To Cecilia, thank you for caring so well for our son when I wasn't a fulltime father and for being my friend.

To my cousin, Alan Tomasetti thank you for giving so selflessly of your time, energy, advice and support in producing videos, and being instrumental with marketing and promotional tools and ideas.

To my aunt Virginia, thank you for taking me to Palisades Amusement Park almost daily in my formative years and for loving and caring for me as my mother did.

To Anthony Terrezza, thank you for making the audio version of the book a possibility through your editing and studio facilities.

To Sharon Upp, Tina Terrezza, and Betsy Warren, thank you all for your support, encouragement and contributions in editing the manuscript.

A heartfelt thanks to the following friends, Edward and Leslie Lerner, Larry North and Marilyn Witt, and Michael and Sharon Upp, for their advice, encouragement and support, and for sharing their love, laughter, good times, excellent food and great drinks. You are all a blessing in my life.

About the Author

Arthur James Tassinello, life and business coach, seminar speaker and award-winning salesperson knows the value of a challenge. He knows because he has first hand experience struggling to find his own way. Arthur studied at McKendree and Rutgers Universities, has worked in corporate America, and owned and operated several businesses. These important aspects of life—the ability to earn a living and to be of value to others—are but only a jumping off point.

Living in a culture that prizes materialism above all else, he accomplish what we all want, financial success. However, he was not completely satisfied. Something else was calling him and his heart knew there was more. Letting his spirit speak he began another journey. That journey of self-assessment leading him to study philosophies of the ages -scientific and spiritual —tried and true systems—that provided a more fulfilling way to experience life. It is this happiness, satisfaction and appreciation for the gift of life that the universe provides is what Arthur wants you to experience.

Today, life seems to becoming more strained and difficult. We see that many hard-working individuals are looking for work. Our financial systems are in a state of flux and so many individuals and corporations are finally realizing that they need to transform the way they act. This is a time to "Shift our consciousness," and as Martin Luther King once said, "The truth will set you free."

Arthur wants you to join him on his personal journey into self-discovery and transformation because, through struggle and experience he has discovered ways to enrich life, experience true happiness and transform relationships.

The universe is calling us and challenging us to be the change needed at this time in our history, more than ever. As Gandhi said, "You must be the change you want to see in the world," because that is the only way change will happen.

I have witnessed the transition in Arthur and can attest to his growth and transformation into living a joyous life. Listen to him he has a valuable message.

Sharon Upp - Author, Ordained Minister, Astrologer and Editor

Preface

Writing "Quantum Shift into Greatness," was a challenge trying to meld scientific with spiritual information for an understanding of how they are in agreement, more so now than at anytime before. While I have taken the path of the universe being created by design, as opposed to by chance, it is up to you to discover and decide for yourself.

The root, or basis of this book is Kabbalah, and The Zohar. What I am sharing with you is a synthesis of these teachings and information from dozens of scientific and spiritual sources as well as from such luminaries as Wayne Dyer, Stuart Wilde, James Arthur Ray, Marianne Williamson and many others.

One thing I can tell you through my experience is that the "Universal Laws," I speak of, have enormous power in your achieving a better life for yourself and for others. By my applying these teachings of the universal laws I was able to manifest this book and a better life. A life that I was meant to have from birth but didn't recognize, and didn't know how to achieve, until now.

I recorded the processes that brought results—the results that can only come by practice, belief and life experience. I noticed how I began to transform into someone more compassionate, more loving and more giving than I had ever been. Not until I realized that I was living proof could I sit down and write about this information and the tools for experiencing such a shift.

While I have proved this to myself, I don't expect you to believe me. I only ask that you use these tools for yourself and discover their power to create a positive shift in your life. Prove it to yourself.

We all have the potential within us to manifest a life that is beautiful, joyful, loving, compassionate, successful and exciting by doing what we are passionate about, for what we do with passion; we do well and in the process, bring joy to others.

Additionally this book is not just for you, it is for everyone. It is for everyone because this is not just about how you can have "Stuff," it's about change for yourself and the world. I call it stuff because most of us want the material "Stuff." I know that you want things, but the truth is, things have a very short shelf life. You get something new and shiny and you're happy for a day, a week, maybe a month? What I want you to have is life-long happiness. What I want for you and you should want for yourself is true happiness, harmony and success with everything and everyone.

Partly, this book is a promotion for world peace. Now you can go, "what?" That's right you and I have that much power, but it doesn't happen overnight and sometimes it only happens one person at a time. However, even one person at a time can be one each day, which means 365 new peacemakers a year just from you. Here's how it works exponentially. On day one, one person makes one new friend. On day two, both you and your new friend make a new friend, this now becomes four. On day three, the four of you each add a friend and that becomes eight and so on, doubling that number each day assuming that each person adds one more friend each day. At the end of 21 days, there will be over one million people who are friends. The actual number is 1,048,576. Do you think it's possible to have peace in one year? Yes I realize that you may think it's not possible and so I say, "What you think you will manifest." If you intend it, it will happen. By the way at the end of 1 month that number is over a billion, 1,073,741,824 to be exact. Anything is possible.

In closing this information will change your life if you do the work and want all the great things the universe has to offer whether you believe in a higher power or not. Have the courage to step out of your box and be passionate about your life. Allow the inherent joy within you to erupt.

See yourself as a success.

Begin now.

Make the Shift! I'm with you.

Quantum Shift into Greatness

Chapter One
Kabbalah

Ancient Wisdom and Mysticism

Kabbalah it is the doorway into the ultimate true reality, which reveals the deepest, most hidden secrets of the universe. The wisdom of Kabbalah is the most ancient of all wisdoms. It goes back 3,800 years to the time of Abraham the Patriarch, in the 18th century BC. You'll find that modern physicists continue to validate its writings.

As with most ancient texts there are many speculations as to where it came from, when it came into being and who authored it. Suffice to say that it is a scientific, time-tested, empirical method of achieving spirituality while living here in this world.

Although many Kabbalists and scholars will disagree on the date of its origins, scholars tend to identify Kabbalah with specific ideas that emerged in 12th century Provence, France in the school of R. Isaac the Blind or also known as Rabbi Yitzhak Saggi Nehor, who has been called "the father of Kabbalah."

One thing that is abundantly clear, from the earliest times, is that there is a continuous thread of Jewish mysticism within its teachings. These strands of mysticism are so intertwined with Kabbalah that it is difficult to know where one ends and another begins. For example, the highly influential text, the Sepher Yetzirah (Book of Creation) was the subject of widespread commentary by medieval Kabbalists, with that text supposedly written as early as the 1st. century. Additionally, ideas from Jewish Gnosticism from the 2nd and 3rd centuries have also become deeply embedded in Kabbalah.

The earliest documents associated with Kabbalah are from the period of approximately 100 to 1000 A.D. These writings describe the attempts of

"Merkabah" mystics to penetrate the seven halls (Hekaloth) of creation to reach the Merkabah (the four-wheeled chariot driven by four "chayot" each of which has four wings and four faces, a man, a lion, an ox, and an eagle) of God. These mystics appear to have used what would now be recognized as familiar methods of shamanism (fasting, repetitious chanting, prayer, posture) to induce a trance state. In the trance state, these mystics literally fought their way past terrible guards and seemingly impenetrable seals to reach an ecstatic state in which they "saw God."

By the early Middle Ages, more theosophical developments had taken place, chiefly the development of an esoteric view of creation as a process in which God manifests in a series of emanations, or sephiroth. The doctrine of the sephiroth can be found in a elementary form in the "Sepher Yetzirah." However, by the time of the publication of the book "Bahir" or "Book of the Brightness" (an anonymous mystical work) in the 12th century it had reached a form not too different from the form it takes today.

Kabbalah is the spiritual heritage of all humankind. It is here to help you on your path to growth, understanding and transformation. Kabbalah transcends and predates any religious identification, ethnicity, nation or country, though the central text of Kabbalah is The Zohar.

No More or Less Radical than Science

Kabbalah is a book of spiritual wisdom and teachings, it is not religious and it is not about your being obedient to certain laws or commandments. Unlike other customs or societies that use inspirational approaches to divine wisdom, Kabbalah is a tool to be used in, and a logical analysis of, spiritual matters. Much like quantum physics, which tell us that electrons can exist in two places at one time or that time may not exist at all, Kabbalah may seem contradictory or even ironic and asks us to accept nothing more radical or less radical than that which we understand from physics.

Many teachings, ancient and modern, derive their knowledge from Kabbalah and The Zohar. Laws that we will discuss later, to further your well-being, come from these works as well. Think of the Kabbalah as a tool, a guide or an application and a conduit to remove doubt and fear and enhance your life. Rather than it being some kind of religious dogma. The Zohar and Kabbalah belong to everyone and are to be used everyday for those who truly desire to grow, learn and transform themselves and their surroundings.

Studying Kabbalah changes your perspective on the world and opens up areas within you that you never knew existed. Kabbalah is a journey of discovery that affects you on all levels, including what you do and how you do it. It influences your relationships with your family, friends, and co-workers. It affects your health, your mind, your spirit, and your wealth. Kabbalah very simply states that when you know how to directly connect to the Creator, without any go-betweens, you will find your inner compass. Kabbalah will help you make, and sustain, direct contact with the Creator. By doing so, you will need no further guidance.

As most of us know or have experienced it is difficult to form new habits and even more difficult to let go of old habits or preconceived notions. Why does it seem so much easier to endure the pain of living in disharmony, or in angst, or in a troubled relationship as we do, than to struggle in transforming ourselves and changing the world?

The Age of Aquarius

Many believe that when the creator put us here it was Her intention to have us experience pain and suffering. However, it is man that beset himself with the troubles we experience, as the creator only wants us to experience love, peace and happiness. Although we are living, and have lived, in some very trying times be assured that this - the Age of Aquarius - is the time in which many of us will see and experience the true love of who we are and share in the beauty of the everlasting Light.

Many people who are not Jewish and have no religious affiliation whatsoever are experiencing Kabbalah today. The true purpose of Kabbalah and why it is being revealed now, as in no other time in history, is to help us understand who we are and what we can do to restore Creation to its originally intended state so we may re-enter the Eden from where we were expelled. While many of these very spiritual and powerful tools we will use are identified with Judaism they are meant for all people of the world.

The Kabbalah explains why we are here, what the future holds, and how we can avoid pain and suffering so we can feel tranquil and safe. It has answers for everything we have questions about. The truth is that we are all motivated by wanting to receive love, delight and pleasure. It is this desire, which motivates all of our actions, thoughts, and feelings, and Kabbalah shows us how we can fulfill our desires and our wishes.

Although the wisdom of Kabbalah often tends to sound technical or obscure, it is important to remember that this is a very sensible science. The people who mastered it and wrote about it were just like you and me. They were seeking solutions to the same questions we all want answered, many of which are found in Kabbalah but more so in ourselves as we read and experience life.

So, Is Kabbalah Jewish?

It is quite understandable that Kabbalah is confused with Judaism. Throughout history, many scholars of Kabbalah have been Jewish; however, there have also been many non-Jewish scholars of this wisdom, such as Christian Knorr-von-Rosenroth, Pico Della Plato, Leone Ebreo, Leonardo da vinci and Sir Isaac Newton, to name a few.

The startling truth is that Kabbalah was never meant for a specific sect, it was intended for use by all humanity to unify the world. Today, millions of people of all faiths have discovered this wisdom and have experienced the powerful effects of studying Kabbalah.

There are two primary reasons why so many people are now interested in

Kabbalah. First, it's that Kabbalah works. When you apply the wisdom and tools of Kabbalah you experience positive results. The second reason why so many people of different faiths have become connected to Kabbalah is that its tools can enhance your life whether you practice a religion or not.

What are the basic teachings of Kabbalah?

Kabbalah helps us recognize the sources of negativity in our own minds and hearts, and teaches how to use the tools for creating positive changes in everything we do, so we can claim the gifts we were created to receive. We earn these gifts by undertaking our spiritual work — the process of fundamentally transforming ourselves.

Kabbalah let's us see that every human being is a work in progress. Any pain, disappointment, or chaos that exists in our lives is not because this is how life was meant to be, but because we have not yet finished the work that brought us here. That work, quite simply, is the process of freeing ourselves from the domination of the ego and creating an affinity with the sharing essence of God.

In practical terms, this transformation means letting go of anger, jealousy, and other reactive behaviors in favor of patience, empathy, and compassion. It does not mean giving up all desire and going to live on a mountaintop. On the contrary, it means desiring more of the fulfillment that humanity was meant to have.

By way of an example, there is the story of the monk who lived for years on a mountaintop. He was so peaceful and spoke with God daily. One day after 13 years of seclusion he descends from the mountaintop and enters the town. In town he meets many people who go to him for answers about how to live their lives and how to have peace and tranquility. As he completes his rounds he enters a store and asks to use the bathroom. The owner replies that if he is not a customer he cannot. The monk who is in great pain at this point turns to the shop owner and knocks him down and proceeds to the bathroom. It is relatively easy to be at peace and loving within yourself when you are alone, but the real test of living is with others. Can you find yourself loving while being in the living?

Nature and Man's Well-Being

As most of us realize, nature works perfectly without the intervention of man because each part of life has its designated function. There is not one part of creation that does not affect the well-being of the other; each part depends on the well-being of all other parts. All creatures of nature are independent and connected with one another, which means that no creature should overpower another creature because to destroy another creature would be the same as destroying itself. We are no exception to this rule, but many do not appreciate this idea or principle; they hurt others and, in doing so, they hurt themselves as well.

As a prime example take those companies that manufacture, sell, and distribute products that they know are not safe so they may make a profit. Is it the company who makes these decisions or is it the people running the company who make the decisions? How is it that these same people believe that they will not be affected by these harmful products? How can they believe that they are outside of this consumptive circle and that these harmful products will not affect their families, friends and co-workers? What you do is one thing; how you do it is another. What you are doing is making a product, of which the profits will support, the people who work there. How you make the product and how it affects others is the crux of a good company. We will all agree that profits are necessary, however greed should not override the obligation of producing a product that will not be harmful to people's lives and health.

Why do we think we can manipulate and shape the world to our liking without some dire consequences? All around us, with just a quick view of the news you see the results. What are we achieving? We are bringing unhappiness upon others and ourselves. We use profits and greed as an excuse to manipulate people and resources, which threatens our environment wreaking havoc and destruction.

Kabbalah is it a Passing Fad?

Kabbalah has been around for a long, long time and is only now taking its place in the general public awareness. It has been waiting in hiding until the questions it answers could arise. Kabbalah has been incorrectly associated with many flavors of spiritual teachings and religions. Well it is not a passing fad, but a time-tested, practical method to understanding human nature and the nature of the Creator. Those who embrace it as the latest fad will perhaps move on to something else; however, those who dig deeply into its principles are likely to find enough to keep them going for a lifetime.

Kabbalah is a system or sequence of methods that help us understand some of life's deepest questions. Kabbalistic wisdom is also a source of intelligence that helps us choose a better way of thinking and acting, which in turn, assists us in creating a better future, because our reality is created from our thoughts.

Finally, here's what Kabbalah is not as is quoted from "A Guide to the Hidden Wisdom of Kabbalah" by Michael Laitman. Kabbalah is not, and has nothing to do with religion, magic, mysticism, divination, cults, holistic medicine, meditation, philosophy, theosophy, psychology or parapsychology, ESP, telepathy, dream interpretation, tarot cards, yoga, red strings, holy water, blessings, past-life regressions, numerology, reiki, channeling, astrology, astral travels or projection, communicating with the dead, out-of-body experiences, voodoo, freemasonry, reflexology, UFO 's, creationism, Sufism or any -ism."

Now, I do not expect you to accept everything I tell you as true although I have experienced true harmony and success from these teachings myself. You should always question everything and believe nothing. Only your results should be the way to measure something to be true or false. By purchasing this book you have invested a tiny sum for an experience of a lifetime. Here you can use this information and do the work to prove to yourself that you can be anything and everything you believe is true for you. Your only additional investment is in knowing that the universe is always on your side.

Tassinello

If this book and this information intrigue you and help you I am honored to have been instrumental in your success. If you are interested in a receiving a much deeper understanding of this science, read all 23 volumes of The Zohar, which I begin to explain in the next chapter.

Chapter Two
The Zohar

A Fountain Head of Spiritual Wisdom

The Zohar is a great book of wisdom and mystical power universally acknowledged as the authoritative work on the Kabbalah. The Zohar is a commentary on the Bible and is a fountainhead of spiritual energy, and a source of metaphysical power that provides explanations for how to bring blessings, protection and well-being into your life. Zohar in Hebrew means "splendor" or "scintillation," and is literally an unlimited resource of brilliant spiritual Light.

The Zohar is not meant to convince you to be or act a certain way, it only asks that you have a trusting heart, an open and receptive mind and a willingness to participate. Like many great spiritual texts of other practices, The Zohar is written in metaphors, parables, and cryptic language - a kind of code, which at first conceals but ultimately reveals the spiritual and scientific forces of the universe.

Physically it is structured as if you are having conversations with a group of friends, or scholars, or spiritual masters. But the far-reaching reality and power of The Zohar transcends the limits of the physical world. As the Kabbalists explain, simply possessing The Zohar brings power, protection, and fulfillment into our lives.

Whether we study The Zohar from reading it in the original Aramaic language or in its English translation, a deep connection to the Creator's Light comes into being. As we gain intimacy and understanding of The Zohar, our consciousness deepens and expands and we grow and evolve spiritually. We become the person we need to be to gain the joy and fulfillment that God intends for us.

There are some who depict The Zohar as simply another "spiritual" text, or an object for academic study and find The Zohar difficult and even forbidding, but what they find was already determined by their own expectations. In contrast to this, the greatest minds in history have found wisdom and enlightenment in The Zohar's pages.

From Pythagoras in ancient Greece, to Sir Isaac Newton in the 17th century, to the architects of physics and biology in the modern era, students have discovered startling information and insights.

The Zohar not only reveals spiritual principles that can assist us in our everyday lives, but it also gives us the power to put those principles into action in every area of our lives, including our relationships, our spiritual work, and to become more healthy even in our businesses and careers.

The Language of The Zohar

As mentioned above The Zohar is written in the ancient language of Aramaic, a sister language to Hebrew that employs Hebrew letters. While Hebrew was the language of the upper classes, Aramaic was the language of the common people. The Zohar's revelation is that all people, regardless of their spiritual level or status, can use this tool of Light.

Above and beyond the importance of the Aramaic language, the individual letters of The Zohar themselves have special significance. In our everyday lives, we're used to thinking of the letters of the English alphabet in purely functional terms. The letters are units that we put together to create words, just as bricks are the units we use to create a wall. We think of both the letters and the bricks in practical rather than spiritual terms, they're small, inert objects that we use to create larger objects.

The difference with these Aramaic letters is that they work in an entirely different way. They are not just functional components to form words, each Aramaic letter is also a channel to a unique form of spiritual energy, which is true whether or not we know how the letter sounds or how it fits into a given word.

The Aramaic alphabet just like The Zohar is a gift for all humanity, not just the few who know the ancient Aramaic languages. It is said that just by scanning the letters, even if you cannot read or understand them, opens an unlimited channel to the Light. The letters alone have the power to bring spiritual wisdom and positive energy into every area of our lives.

Think of the Aramaic text like it is an electrical current. Like an electrical current running through the conducting wires it cannot be seen, yet it does reveal itself as the light in a bulb or as a heat source. Like electricity, the spiritual Light of the Creator is wrapped, not in cables or wires, but in metaphor and imagery throughout the Aramaic text.

A Wellspring of Spiritual Energy

The Zohar not only reveals and explains spiritual truths; it literally brings blessings, protection, and well-being into the lives of all who come into its presence. Nothing is required, just worthy desire, the certainty of a trusting heart, and an open and receptive mind. The Zohar's ultimate purpose is to bring understanding of life and show us how we can have complete fulfillment. It is an opportunity for us to transform our natures, which is why all the teachings of Kabbalah exist.

Let me be very clear about the purpose of The Zohar as a valuable tool and bridge between everyday consciousness and our inner transformative powers. We live a shallow life where the trappings of the ego invite us to only experience the earthly pleasures. Through The Zohar we can draw in the Light of the creator in revealing the Light in all of us. As we connect to the upper dimensions we eliminate darkness and chaos and experience the knowing of our journey. When studying the English translation of The Zohar, we get information. When scanning the Aramaic text, we also acquire wisdom and a certain inner peace. Scanning the text will summon, from above, spiritual power and Light.

The Zohar is a very powerful tool for cleansing the soul and as a tool for successfully navigating the spiritual road. It helps us in removing darkness and ultimately attaining the transformation that is the true purpose of our lives and enlightenment, bringing blessings and wealth to all. It's a tool to be used everyday not just once a week, by going to some religious institution, only to forget why we go there within minutes after leaving. It is unimportant whether you read a few words, a passage or several pages of The Zohar each day, for just reading it will remind you of your purpose in this life.

Putting Together Pieces of the Puzzle

There are key pieces of awareness from The Zohar to help us in our growth and to gain a better understanding and perspective to know what to do to protect us from the evil that exists in this world. For example there are three distinct energy forces permeating all of existence. Using the language of metaphor, The Zohar identifies these three factors as Right, Left and Central columns.

The Right column is the male influence and the physical expression of water. This right column correlates to the positive (+) force, which manifests itself as the proton of an atom. The left column is the female influence and the physical expression of fire. The left column correlates to the negative (-) force, which manifests itself as the electron of an atom. Wind is the personification of the Central column, or neutral energy, which corresponds to the neutron of an atom - the force that bridges the positive and negative poles. Just as an atom unites these three forces into the building blocks of our physical universe, we, through our actions can unite them as the building blocks of our spiritual universe.

Even scientists agree that atoms make up everything in the universe, from houses, to cars, to trees, to plants, to animals, the sea, air and land. Because everything is made up of atoms, we are all physically connected. Our left side corresponds to the negative pole and to our desire to receive; the right side corresponds to the positive pole or the will to share that, which resides in our soul.

Free Will

Through our free will we can choose to practice self-judgment, as opposed to judging others, and to share, or we can choose to receive from the physical material reality. We can choose to resist the desire to receive and instead to nurture the desire to share. Each of us has the opportunity to fully evolve the good nature within our souls and we must be responsible for our own elevation and growth. We may use our free will for whatever we please, just try and use it for the benefit of all and not just for self-serving interests. Similar to the movie "Pay it Forward" you have an opportunity to always be benevolent, for as you sow, so shall you reap.

Unfortunately, there are people whose sole purpose is to prevent the dissemination of spiritual wisdom because they do not believe in a higher power. Others may believe but they build schools of religious study that hide the truth that we are all capable of practicing good deeds and sharing on our own without being told to do so. While believing differently from someone else does not make you a bad person; however it does make it more difficult for us to see that each of us must do our part individually, as well as collectively. Each of us has the knowledge to differentiate that, which is good from that, which is evil and we know when we are receiving selfishly or giving and sharing for the betterment of humankind. We cannot leave it up to those who believe they are closer to God, or the Light or to whomever you call a higher power, to do our work in this world. Each of us must be our own master and practice living in harmony with each other every day.

The Messiah and Idolatry

There are many who tell us that the Messiah is coming, someone who will heal the world and bring us universal peace. But no one knows when or if, so while you are waiting why not do something. The reality is that we cannot and should not sit on the sidelines waiting for anything. It is within us, and our own spiritual actions, that we will accelerate the arrival of universal peace and immortality by being pro-active now.

There is a passage in the bible that tells us that we should not worship any idols. An idol is defined as any material possession or external situation that controls our emotions, our behavior and our motivation. Idolatry does not just pertain to man-made statues and icons; an idol can be any material item such as a car or house or any such circumstance, which determines or influences our experience of life. If we practice idol worship, then we have surrendered control and severed our connection to the Light - the true source of fulfillment. It is our own negative tendencies that lead us to become worshippers of wealth or disciples of our own ego. You can like money and cars and houses, but don't make them all that you are living for, as it will only bring you sadness in the end.

Bloodshed isn't Just Murder

Most of us would consider murder as one of the most horrendous and outrageous crimes; however, cold-blooded killing does not just refer to bloodshed. Bloodshed occurs when we publicly or privately disgrace or humiliate others, causing blood to rush to their face in embarrassment. While killing someone brings death, it is humiliation and disgrace, which brings a lifetime of hurt to the living. Instead of re-acting to a situation that will cause embarrassment to you or another take a moment to think about what was said and the right way to act. Just as a bell reacts by ringing when the button is pushed, how many times have you done something unkind as a reaction to someone pushing your button? When we react by saying things that disgrace or humiliate another we start wars, we put ourselves at odds with each other and cause a lifetime of injury. Remove your bell and throw away the button. It serves no purpose.

Although it is easy to say, "Well I'm not perfect," as an excuse to act badly, can't we take a moment to try and be better? We all have our boundaries, which includes our own personal physical space. That space where we feel intruded upon when someone gets to close. Though we must consider and respect the boundaries of all people, we still need to exchange ideas and debate with others, provided it is for the sake of peace and goodwill and not for ego gratification. When dialogue takes place with sharing and mutual respect, it adheres to the adage, "The whole is greater than the sum of its parts."

Reincarnation and Existence

Do you believe in reincarnation? Well if you do, you know that each of us chose to be here at this time to perfect ourselves. Many of the crises that confront us in life are from spiritual baggage, the misdeeds in previous incarnations. Incomplete spiritual corrections not achieved in one life are carried over to the next. We can connect to our previous incarnations and make spiritual corrections simply by meditating with the intention to do so. Many people in your life today have been with you in previous lives and each are here to assist us in correcting past issues. If you see it this way it may make it easier for you to see the message and make those corrections.

So let's say you don't believe in reincarnation, it's okay. Just know this that there is a message for you in every situation, and with every one you meet, especially with those with whom you have the most difficult time. Do not miss out on those opportunities to decipher those messages and to use them to reach a higher plain of understanding by recognizing your part and your lessons.

To begin to understand "Universal Laws" you must first understand why the universe exists. While the universe has existed for millions of years, as we know it, mankind has only been around for thousands of years. While science and physicists don't agree on when the beginning came about or how it all began, most agree on the "Big Bang" theory. For those who are spiritual the belief is that, in the beginning the Light or the Source was all that there was and nothing else existed. The substance of the universe only consisted of energy and the Light; there was no opposition. In other words there was no duality, such as black and white, left and right, up and down or good and bad.

From a spiritual perspective, the Light knew itself to be all powerful and infinite living in a realm of absolute. The Light needed something to compare itself with or against for an experience to occur. Thus it divided itself into an infinite number of life forms, hence the "Big Bang."

Let's compare this to a living vessel, which keeps receiving, but never returns what it is receiving. The vessel is complete and perfect. The vessel has only to "be" and enjoy what it receives. However, the vessel wanted to experience giving. So the vessel shatters itself into millions of pieces, or life forms, so each piece of itself could experience giving to itself. In essence our creation was born out of a desire to know itself. So when we say God or the Light is everywhere it literally means God is everywhere, for there is nowhere where God is not.

Chapter Three
What defines us?

The word, define means to give definition for the meaning of a word, to determine the essential quality of, to determine the nature of. What I'm really talking about here is not just how you define yourself but when you meet someone how do you define them?

For many of us we typically define someone, or ourselves, by the way he or she looks. He/she has blue eyes, dark hair, slender and short, etc. If we can get beyond someone's physicality, or looks, then we can use some other quantifiable means of defining and further describing them. However, in describing someone we usually add judgments about him or her, judgments that make comparisons to ourselves. If someone doesn't fit our idea of what's acceptable we further judge their value by what they do or by what they have accomplished and in many cases by the material things they have. So many times we equate having material things with success and we typically see a successful person as someone to be admired and respected. It is interesting that we begin defining someone by their outward appearance and rarely by their actions - how they show up, how they do things, what they do for others, or how they treat other people.

Human history is often defined as the struggle of one group to establish some dominance over another group. Although we can often define ourselves by our differences, such as how we dress, where we live, and our possessions, the real distinction does not lie in these differences, but in the way we treat our fellow humans. It is the degree of humanity in our relationship to others that decides how far we have traveled to make an ideal world of civilized beings that truly have learned and know the art of peaceful coexistence.

Perhaps it's time to reassess how you think of others when you meet them. Will you finally take time get to know someone or will you continue to make those snap judgments and perhaps miss out on making a real connection and learning something. Try to look beyond physical appearances and see the person inside. You might like what you see.

Who Are You Really?

In getting back to the word "define" as to determine the nature and quality of something or someone, I asked if you could define yourself? Do you know how to define yourself? Do you look at all of your material possessions, how well known you are or by what you do? Or will you define yourself as a father or a mother, a husband or a wife, an engineer or a salesman, or as handsome or ugly, or short or tall, or slender or heavy or, or, or anything but who you really are.

The reality is this; you are not how others see you, but who you are. Look at your relationships - how you treat others, if you are there for others, how you act toward others, or your attitude and compassion for others. Can you tell me who you are then? Don't look in the mirror to tell me who you are. Look at how you act and how you do things in the world.

As I heard James Arthur Ray say, "It is not what you do but how you do it." The "How" is the qualifier. While there are many who do "What" you do, it is the "How" that makes the difference. That is why so few people are successful. It is because they do things without making the distinction between what and how. How well will you do things from now on?

Have you have ever seen the reality show where they ask several chefs to make a dish from a few ingredients they are given? Have you noticed what makes the difference in the meal they are preparing? Since they all receive the same ingredients, it can only come down to how they used the ingredients, how they displayed the foods and the presentation? While it seems that they all do the same thing, it is the "How" they do it that sets them apart. One more thing, it also comes down to how passionate they are about what they do.

All in all it is our actions, not our words or beliefs that define us. It is our lack of compassion, care and love that blinds us in denying others of their basic rights. To this point the philosopher Karl Popper was asked in an interview if he believed in evil. "No," he answered, "but I believe in stupidity." Often in Buddhist teachings, the wise are associated with righteousness, and the foolish or ignorant with evil doing. Of course smart or stupid, foolish or ignorance have little to do with acting out of kindness.

Understanding Who You Are

To understand and to know who you are, you must be aware of your actions. You cannot simply say this is who I am if you don't observe yourself. Observe your actions, really look at how you act, think about what people say about you and finally dig deep and admit to those truths about yourself. You may have heard this saying "Do what I say, not what I do." How foolish that you would act one way and ask someone else to act differently. How often do you do this with your children? Unfortunately we all have a tendency to do this in the early stages of life. Isn't it time to act, as you would have others act?

As an example, a few decades ago I got passed over for a promotion and a raise, not because I didn't accomplish the tasks of the job but because of how I accomplished it. I didn't recognize that I was not being a team player. Sure I got the job done but at what cost. The real cost was not respecting others opinions and in turn not earning the respect I thought I should have received for getting the job done. This was far more costly to me than the bottom line of sales and profits and getting the job done. It was a valuable lesson.

The Universal Laws that I will introduce to you in the next section are intended to help you in creating a harmonious life, not just for creating monetary wealth. The messages are here for you to find your passion and true path. They are here for you to develop a greater awareness, intelligence and conscience so you live within the laws of morality, integrity and benevolence.

Tassinello

Chapter Four
Quantum Physics and Theory

What's It All About?

Quantum physics is a branch of science that deals with discrete, indivisible units of energy called quanta as described by the Quantum Theory. There are five main ideas represented in Quantum Theory:

1. Energy is not continuous, but comes in small but discrete units.

2. The elementary particles behave both like particles and like waves.

3. The movement of these particles is inherently random.

4. It is physically impossible to know both the position and the momentum of a particle at the same time. The more precisely one is known, the less precise the measurement of the other is.

5. The atomic world is nothing like the world we live in.

6. What you observe is ever changing, so what you observe is never what you think it is except at the moment of observation.

While this may seem like just another strange theory, quantum physics contains many clues as to the fundamental nature of the universe and is more important then even relativity in the grand scheme of things. Furthermore, it describes the nature of the universe as being much different then the world we see.

We find ourselves living in a very strange and bewildering world, a place where we so desperately want to make sense of everything. We want to know the root of our existence and we want unequivocal proof. Even those who profess to have faith and a belief in a higher power usually want proof as well. We want to know who we are and what our place is in the world. Well, I'm not sure we will ever be able to answer all the questions man has posed, let alone have unequivocal proof, but this is a beginning into this realm as seen through the eyes of scientists and physicists.

Theories – Glue or Tortoises

Scientists, philosophers, mystics, sages, theorists, philosophers and more all have theories of the beginnings and the workings of the universe. We speculate about mans purpose and possibilities. Throughout time there have been all sorts of conjectures about the universe from a tower of tortoises supporting a flat earth and that superstrings exist, yet no one has seen either. Of course we know that tortoises don't uphold the earth, but we also lack observational evidence of superstrings.

This book includes a great deal of material - perhaps more than you want need or care about; however, my quest is to provide information that is more meaningful and comprehensive to tie all of the bits and pieces together as elegantly as possible.

Ideas, speculation, conjecture, assumptions, supposition and outright guessing using math and tests to try and get the answers we all want. Proof that there exists a supreme power. While this section speaks a lot about the science of the universe to give credence to what we believe is true it will come close but there still is no scientific proof of the existence or lack of existence of a higher power.

Why do we have such great difficulty to believe or put faith in anything that cannot be proven scientifically? In the scientific world theories will always come and go, but I nonetheless believe, you will find direct connections between what quantum physicists; chaos theorists, biologists and ancient sages and teachers have been telling us for centuries. And I know that many of you already feel this connection in your core. It is that we exist whether theoretically or physically and that it is important to recognize that, even while there is little tangible evidence, science and spirituality are getting closer to an agreement on there being something greater than man.

Whether we all believe the same thing or not one thing is abundantly clear and that is we must learn to live together to, as Spock on Star Trek would say, "Live long and prosper." As Richard Feynman said "In this book I present perspectives from several teachers and scientists on how nature behaves. If you will simply admit that maybe she does behave like this, you will find her a delightful, entrancing thing. Do not keep saying to yourself but how can it be like that? Because you will get . . . into a blind alley from which nobody has yet escaped. Nobody knows how it can be like that."

Expanding Science and Philosophy

First and foremost science tells us that the universe is infinite and that it is expanding. That should give you pause for thought for it totally changed the discussion on the origin of the universe. You may wish to explore other profound theories that are currently influencing the worlds of science and philosophy. For example I present to you how Thomas Knierim explains science and philosophy as I quote directly from his website at www.thebigview.com.

Natural science has always had a great influence on philosophy and on the way we see the world. Until the age of the Renaissance there was no clear distinction between philosophy and science. Speculations about physics and astronomy were among the favorite topics of the natural philosophers of antiquity and continued to flourish until the time of Copernicus. The desire to explore the starry heavens and to reveal its secrets is probably as old as mankind itself. However, notable advances in this discipline were made only fairly recently, after the invention of the telescope in the 17th century. This section deals with the accomplishments of 20th century physics in the world of the largest structures, such as galaxies and stars, and that of the smallest structures, such as atoms and particles. This chapter takes a closer look at Relativity and Quantum Physics in particular, both of which have given us amazing new insights into what we call creation.

Newton: The Three Laws of Motion

According to physics, the world used to be a predictable place. Aristotle and Ptolemy laid the foundation for the scientific understanding of the universe, which remained authoritative for one-and-a-half thousand years. Until the time of Galileo, the Greeks were undisputed in natural science and astronomy. Galileo, Copernicus, and Newton changed this. Isaac Newton (1642-1727) revolutionized physics with his proposition that the three laws of motion govern all bodies. The first law of motion states that a body continues in a state of rest or continues to be moving uniformly in a straight line unless a force is applied to the object. The second law states that the force applied to an object is proportional to its mass multiplied by acceleration ($F=ma$). The third law states that for every action there is an equal opposite reaction.

With these three simple laws, Newton created a whole new model of the universe, superseding Ptolemy's model of epicycles. Eighty years before, Galileo (1564-1642) had pointed out that the Earth rotates around the Sun. The mechanics developed by Newton and Galileo provided the basis for 17th to 19th century cosmology. In this view, planets revolved in well-defined orbits around stars, where the gravitational force balances the rotational force. According to the universal law of gravitation, bodies attract each other with a force $F=m1*m2/r^2$, which means that the force increases with mass and decreases (squared) with distance.

Laplace: The Mechanistic Universe

Given these natural laws, mankind derived a picture of the universe that accounts neatly for mass, position, and the motion of the celestial bodies. Further, these celestial bodies are seen as dynamic elements of a celestial apparatus, not unlike that of a mechanical apparatus; thus it is called a mechanistic worldview. The mechanistic worldview was illustrated in its purest form by Marquis de Laplace (1749-1827) in his writing Mécanique Céleste. The mechanistic view sees the universe as an arrangement in which stars and planets interact with each other like springs and cogs in a clockwork, while God is watching from above. If the initial positions and states of all objects in a mechanically determined universe are known, all events can be predicted until the end of time, simply by applying the laws of mechanics. It was further thought that this kind of knowledge is available only to an omniscient God.

The mechanistic view does not make any statements about the creation of the universe, because according to this view creation was pre-established by God. From a mechanistic standpoint, solar systems like our own are in a delicate balance, because only a slight increase or decrease in mass or velocity of the planets would let the planets either spiral into the Sun or wander into outer space. There had to be a construction plan. Thus the necessity for a creator God arose to also explain the universe was initially balanced. Needless to say that the church was comfortable with this theory, despite the earlier quarrels with Galileo, and in spite of the fact that it generally viewed scientific progress with great suspicion.

One of the most enthralling aspects of Relativity is its revolutionary understanding of time. The term "time dilation" might evoke images of Salvadore Dali's timepieces hanging on twigs; however, time dilation is all but surrealistic. The Theory of Relativity states that if the speed of light is constant, time cannot be constant. In fact, it doesn't make sense to speak of time as being constant or absolute, when we think of it as one dimension of space-time. Special Relativity states, that time is measured according to the relative velocity of the reference frame in which it is measured. Despite of the simplicity of this statement, the relativistic connection between time and space are hard to fathom.

The Four Dimensions of Space-Time

In the Relativity Theory the world has four dimensions: three space dimensions and one dimension that is not exactly time but related to time. In fact, it is time multiplied by the square root of -1. Imagine you are moving from point A to point B through one space dimension. When you move to another space coordinate, you automatically cause your position on the time coordinate to change, even if you don't notice, which causes time to elapse. Of course, you are always traveling through time, but when you travel through space you travel through time more slowly than you expect. The well-known following example of the "twin paradox" demonstrates the time dilation phenomenon.

Time Dilation; the Twin Paradox

Consider the case of these twin brothers. On their thirtieth birthday, one of the brothers goes on a space journey in a super fast rocket that travels at 99% of the speed of light. The space traveler stays on his journey for precisely one year, whereupon he returns to Earth on his 31st birthday. Because time is stretched by a factor of 7 at approximately 99% of the speed of light, in the space one year is equivalent to seven years on earth. Therefore seven years have actually elapsed, so his twin, the space travelers' brother is 37 years old at the time of his return. Yet, time appears to have passed normally to both brothers, i.e. both still need five minutes to shave each morning in their respective reference frame.

According to the Theory of Relativity, we learn that time and space is seemingly independent of human experience, as suggested by the example of time dilation. However, since our own perception of time and space is bound to a single reference frame, time appears to be constant and absolute to us. Physics teaches us that this constancy is an illusion and that our perception deceived us within living memory. Thanks to Einstein, we are now able to draw relativistic space-time diagrams, compute gravitational fields, and predict trajectories through the four-dimensional space-time continuum. However, we are barely able to visualize this space-time continuum, or deal with it in practical terms, because human consciousness is bound to the human body, which is in turn bound to a single reference frame. We live within the confinements of our own space-time cubicle.

Quantum Theory in the Twentieth Century

Now let's consider the Quantum theory, which evolved as a new branch of theoretical physics during the first few decades of the 20th century in an endeavor to understand the fundamental properties of matter. In contrast to Einstein's Relativity, which is concerned with the largest things in the universe, quantum theory deals with the tiniest things we know, the particles that atoms are made of, which we call "subatomic" particles.

Just as light is thought to have a dual nature, sometimes showing the characteristic of a wave, and sometimes that of a particle (photon), quantum theory attributes a similar dual wave-particle nature to subatomic particles. Electrons that orbit around the nucleus interact with each other by showing interference patterns, not unlike those of wave interference. If the velocity of the electron is thought of as its wavelength, the crests of neighboring electron waves amplify or cancel each other, thereby creating a pattern that corresponds to Bohr's allowed orbits.

The nature of electrons seems odd; they exist in different places at different points in time. However, it is impossible to say where the electron will be at a given time. At time t1 it is at point A, then at time t2 it is at point B, yet the electron has not actually moved from A to B. It seems to appear in different places without describing a trajectory. Therefore, even if t1 and A can be pinpointed, it is impossible to derive t2 and B from this measurement. In other words: There seems to be no causal relation between any two positions. The concept of causality cannot be applied to what is observed. In case of the electrons of an atom, the closest we can get to describe the electron's position is by giving a number for the probability of it being at a particular place. Moreover, particles have other "disturbing" properties: They have a tendency to decay into other particles or into energy, and sometimes -under special circumstances- they merge to form new particles. Which occurs after indeterminate time spans. Although we can make statistical assertions about a particle's lifetime, it is impossible to predict the fate of an individual particle.

Does It Matter or Not?

Can we derive any new knowledge about the universe from quantum physics? After all, the entire universe is composed of an unimaginable large number of matter and energy. Quantum theory can only be understood in view of the large-scale structure of the cosmos. For example, one might ask is why the observable matter in the universe is packed together in galaxies and rather than being evenly distributed throughout space. Could it have to do with the quantum characteristics of energy? Are quantum effects responsible for matter forming discrete entities, instead of spreading out evenly during the birth of the universe? The answer to this question is still being debated.

Physics and Eastern Philosophy

Though cosmological conclusions seem labored, we may be able to derive philosophical insights from quantum physics. Fritjof Capra ponders this philosophical possibility in his book The Tao of Physics where he describes the parallels between modern physics and ancient Eastern philosophy. He posits that in a way, the essence of modern physics is comparable to the teachings of the ancient Eastern philosophies, such as the Chinese Tao Te Ching, the Indian Upanishads, or the Buddhist Sutras. Eastern philosophies agree that ultimate reality is indescribable and unapproachable, not only in terms of common language, but also in the language of mathematics. In other words, both science and mathematics fail in describing ultimate reality. This fact is exemplified in the Uncertainty Principle, which is elucidated in the following section.

The oriental scriptures agree that all observable and describable realities are manifestations of the same underlying "divine" principle. Although many phenomena of the observable world are seemingly unrelated, they all go back to the same source; they are intertwined and interdependent to an unfathomable degree, just as the particles in an atom are. Although the electrons in an atom can be thought of as individual particles, they are not really individual particles, because of the complicated wave relations that exist between them.

Hence, the electron cloud model describes the atomic structure more adequately. The sum of electrons in an atom cannot be separated from its nucleus, which has a compound structure itself and can neither be regarded a separate entity. Thus, there is unity in the multiplicity; matter is many things and one thing at the same time.

Eastern scriptures say that no statement about the world is ultimately valid ("The Tao that can be told is not the eternal Tao." Tao Te Ching, Verse 1), because not even the most elaborate language, including the language of science, is capable of rendering a perfect model of the universe. Science is often compared to a tree that branches out into many directions, with physics following the tree upward to its branches and leaves. However meta-physics follows it down to the roots. Whether the branches of knowledge stretch out indefinitely is still a matter of debate. However, it appears that most scientific discoveries do not only answer questions, but also raise new ones.

Relativity and Quantum Theory

Relativity and quantum theory remain inconsonant to the present day, despite great efforts to create a unified theory capable of accommodating both views. After having published his papers on Relativity, Einstein dedicated the rest of his life to working on such a unified field theory, without success. The physicists who followed his lead developed a new model called string theory during the 1970s and 1980s. String theory is successful to some extent in providing a mathematical model that integrates the strong and the weak nuclear forces, electromagnetism, and gravitation. In spite of this, it cannot yet be called a breakthrough, because the theory has not been corroborated thoroughly by observational evidence; and there is not one, but five competing string theories. The latter point has recently been addressed by M-theory, a theory that unites existing string theories in 11 dimensions. Scientists talk about the existence of The Zero Point Field, which is a vast inexhaustible quantum ocean of energy whose subatomic particles ceaselessly pass packets of energy back and forth. What is so interesting about these particles is that they can be anything and can change into anything at any given moment, because they exist in a state of possibility and potential. Thus, in essence reality is what we choose it to be. Additionally, until the 20th century the universe was thought to be constant in time. Although these particles seem to be much the same at each position in space, they are definitely changing in time.

Puzzling Universe

The great physicist Stephen Hawkings also speaks of these quirks and quarks. Hawkings makes other statements about if stars had been radiating for an infinite time, they would have heated up the universe to their temperature. In this scenario, even at night the whole sky would be as bright as the sun, because every line of sight would either end on a star or on a cloud of dust that had been heated up until it was as hot as the stars. Here is where science and spirituality meet. If stars had been sitting there forever, why did they suddenly light up just a few thousand years ago? What was the clock that suddenly told them to shine? This question has puzzled many philosophers who have believed the universe existed forever. However, for most lay people, it was consistent with the idea that the universe had been created a few thousand years ago.

Spirituality and the Big Bang

Here is more food for more thought. Hubble discovered something even more fascinating and remarkable. He learned that by analyzing light astronomers could measure whether other galaxies are moving toward or away from us. To their surprise they found that nearly all galaxies are moving away from us; thus the universe is expanding, which goes along with the spiritual and scientific theory of the "Big Bang."

Is matter an illusion? Is the universe floating on a vast sea of light, whose invisible power provides the resistance that gives to matter its feeling of solidity? Astrophysicist Bernhard Haisch and his colleagues have followed the equations to some compelling -- and provocative conclusions.

In paticular, Haisch's work Brilliant Disguise: Light, Matter and the Zero-Point Field points out how wondrous, complicated and spiritual life is.

"God Said, "Let There Be Light," and There Was Light."

The statement, "Let there be light, and there was light" certainly is a beautiful poetic statement, but does it contain any science? A few years ago Haisch would have dismissed that possibility. As an astrophysicist, he knew all too well the blatant contradictions between the sequence of events in Genesis and the physics of the Universe. Even after substituting eons for days, the order of events was obviously wrong. It made no sense to have light come first, and then to claim that the Sun, the moon and the stars — the obvious sources of light in the night sky of the ancient world — were created only subsequently, be it days or eons later. One could, of course, generalize light to mean simply energy, and thus claim a reference to the Big Bang, but that would be more of a stretch than a revelation.

Haisch's first inkling that the deceptively simple "Let there be light" might actually contain a profound cosmological truth came in early July 1992. He was trying to wrap things up in his Palo Alto office so he could spend the rest of the summer doing research on the X-ray emission of stars at the Max Planck Institute in Garching, Germany. He came in one morning just before his departure and found a rather peculiar message on the answering machine; it had been left at 3 a.m. by Alfonso Rueda, a professor at California State University in Long Beach. Rueda was so excited by the results of a horrifically long mathematical analysis he had been grinding through that he just had to tell Haisch about it.   What Rueda had succeeded in doing was to derive the equation: $F=ma$. Details would follow in Germany.

The Zero-Point Field

To understand it, consider a grandfather clock with its pendulum swinging back and forth. If you don't wind the clock, friction will sooner or later bring the pendulum to a halt. Now imagine a pendulum that gets smaller and smaller, so small that it ultimately becomes atomic in size and subject to the laws of quantum physics. There is a rule in quantum physics called the 'Heisenberg Uncertainty Principle' that states that no quantum object, such as a microscopic pendulum, can ever be brought completely to rest. Any microscopic object will always possess a residual random *jiggle* thanks to quantum fluctuations.

Radio, television and cellular phones all operate by transmitting or receiving electromagnetic waves. Visible light is the same thing; it is just a higher frequency form of electromagnetic waves. At even higher frequencies, beyond the visible spectrum, you find ultraviolet light, X-rays and gamma rays. All are electromagnetic waves, which are really just different frequencies of light.

In quantum theory, the Heisenberg is routinely applied to electromagnetic waves, since electric and magnetic fields flowing through space oscillate like a pendulum. A tiny bit of electromagnetic jiggling will always be present in every possible frequency. If you add up all these ceaseless fluctuations, what you get is a background sea of light with an enormous amount of energy - the zero-point field. While the "zero-point" energy is huge, it is the lowest possible energy state. All other energy is over and above the zero-point state. Take any volume of space and take away everything else — in other words, create a vacuum — and what you are left with is the zero-point field. We can imagine a true vacuum, devoid of everything, but the zero-point field with its ceaseless electromagnetic waves permeates the real-world quantum vacuum.

The fact that the zero-point field is the lowest energy state makes it unobservable. We see things by way of contrast. The eye works by letting light fall on the otherwise dark retina. But if the eye were filled with light, there would be no darkness to provide a contrast. The zero-point field is such a blinding light. Since it is everywhere, inside and outside of us, permeating every atom in our bodies, we are effectively blind to it. The world of light that we do see is all the rest of the light that is over and above the zero-point field.

The World is an Illusion

The work that Rueda, Haisch and another colleague, Hal Puthoff, have since done indicate that mass is, in effect, an illusion. To put it in somewhat *metaphysical terms*, there exists *a background sea of quantum light filling the universe*. This light generates a force that opposes acceleration when you push on any material object, which is why matter seems to be the solid stable stuff that our world is made of. The solid, stable world of matter appears to be sustained at every instant by an underlying sea of quantum light.

Further, in the reference frame of light, there is no space and time. If we look up at the Andromeda galaxy in the night sky, we see light that, from our point of view took 2 million years to traverse the vast distance of space. But to a beam of light radiating from some star in the Andromeda galaxy, the transmission from its point of origin to our eye seems instantaneous.

There must be a deeper meaning in these physical facts, a deeper truth about the simultaneous interconnection of all things. The possibility of profound meaning pushes us forward in our search for a better, truer understanding of the nature of the universe, and the origins of space and time — those "illusions" that feel so real to us, which brings us to one last consideration that will confound and enlighten us: string theory.

Which Dimension Are you Living In?

String theory is of interest to many physicists because it requires new mathematical and physical ideas to mesh together its very different mathematical formulations. One of the most inclusive of these ideas is the 11-dimensional M-theory. M-theory requires space-time to have eleven dimensions, as opposed to the usual three dimensions of space and one of time. The original string theories from the 1980s describe special cases of M-theory where the eleventh dimension is a very small circle or a line. If these original formulations are considered fundamental, then string theory must have ten dimensions. The theory also describes universes like ours, with four observable space-time dimensions, as well as universes with up to 10 flat space dimensions. This theory also provides for cases where the position in some of the dimensions is not described by a real number, but by completely different type of mathematical quantity. Thus, in string theory, space-time dimension is not fixed; it is actually different in different circumstances.

If You Want Proof Look Inside

So why have I brought all this scientific information to you? As I said earlier I want you to see that not even science has an answer for everything. Although we desire proof of almost everything, proof is elusive and ever changing, whether it is directly questioning science or questioning the existence of God. Is it possible we have found the proof but continue to be in denial, because we cannot fathom anything as incredible and amazing as a God or the Light?

Paradoxically, The Zohar states that although Light enables us to see, it is invisible. When a beam of light strikes an object in the darkness we see the object and perhaps the resistance it meets, but we don't see the beam of light itself. Take a flashlight and shine it in complete darkness and you will only see the beam of light as it reflects off of things that it strikes. It could be a large object or dust in the air, however if it is placed in a vacuum you will see nothing.

Would being able to remember our past incarnations provide more understanding? How many lifetimes have you lived? Where were you before this life and where will you go? When will you get to wherever it is you are going? How will you know when you get there and then what will you do? These questions will always be and have always been; so listen to your inner voice, for it has all the answers. You are *"The Universe in a Nutshell"* as Stephen Hawkings titled his book. Are we not each a universe in our own nutshell? Likewise, though science has provided us with so many amazing discoveries, we still know so little about the universe and about ourselves.

On the other hand we really do know a lot about ourselves intuitively. We know that we need and want love, food, shelter and companionship. So is this termed a physical need or a spiritual need? Perhaps it's a little of both. The fact is that you can't buy love, compassion, empathy or any of those things you feel can you? Science can't find these attributes anywhere and certainly can't measure them, can they?

So then why are we so opposed to believing something greater could exist? Is it that we don't want to know? Or if we do put faith in anything but ourselves we will become vulnerable in some way? Maybe we just don't want to know that there are universal laws that we should be living by, because then many of us would wind up in spiritual jail? I may jest a bit and infuse some logic as well, but the facts remain, that no one can tell you unequivocally anything so why not have some faith and trust in something.

Quantum Physics Synopsis:

- Many physicists, biologists, and theorists agree with what ancient teachers and wise men have been telling us since ancient times, there may be a higher power.

- The mathematics of physics postulates that the universe is comprised of 10, probably 11 dimensions.

- Everything is energy from your car, to your home, to your clothes, all of nature and you. We're all made of the same stuff.

- What differentiates one thing from another is the rate at which it vibrates.

- Time does not exist. Everything is happening simultaneously right now.

- You create your past and future in the present. Remember the present is "a present."

- Even in a vacuum there is a ceaseless random *jiggle*.

- 95% of the universe itself is vibrating so fast that everything you can't see is called dark matter.

- The solid, stable world of matter appears to be sustained, at every instant by an underlying sea of quantum light.

- Because the universe is expanding it seems to verify the spiritual and scientific hypothesis of the "Big Bang Theory."

- Electrons seem to exist in different places at different points in time, yet it is impossible to say where the electron will be at a given time.

Chapter Five
Science and Spirituality

Perhaps the information on The Zohar and Kabbalah will not seem so odd or queer now that you know that scientific tenets are not so different. These tenets, which establish the foothold necessary before you, begin climbing the mountain. It's like trying to play a game with no rules. You need to know from the beginning what the rules of the game are so you can measure how you're doing. Though we already have the spiritual information in our soul from birth, some need guidelines that allow them to gauge if they are going in the right direction.

Fritz-Albert Popp is a German researcher in biophysics whose studies also validate how we create our own reality. Biophotons, first discovered in 1923 by Professor Alexander G.Gurvich, who named them "mitogenetic rays." Since the 1970s biophotons have been rediscovered and validated by ample experimental and theoretical evidence. In 1974 Fritz-Albert Popp has proved their existence, their origin from the DNA and their coherence or laser-like nature. Popp expanded biophoton theory to explain biophotons' possible biological in controlling biochemical processes, growth, differentiation etc. Popp's biophoton theory provides many startling insight, including what may be a major element into the life processes and may well provide one of the major elements of a future theory of life and holistic medical practice.

Lynne McTaggart wrote a book called "The Quest for the Secret Force of the Universe" which points to evidence of the quantum energy field within our bodies and all living matter. I mention it because we continually discover and amass more and more evidence of an energy field that is so complex and so very sophisticated in how it communicates with all the cells of living creatures, how light and rhythms plays a role within the body and our DNA, and how the rate of biophoton emissions goes up to restore a patients equilibrium and how these missions act as sort of correction by a living system in the Zero Point Field fluctuations.

If you are familiar with Eastern and Chinese medicine this may be familiar to you. This is a Chinese philosophical principle of the holistic nature of the universe, where humans are essentially a representation of the universe. For example, the heart is like the sun in the sky, the lungs the atmosphere or the sky itself, the digestion is the soil of the earth and the kidneys are the salty oceans.

Scientific studies after studies continually validate the existence of communication not only within our bodies but also between us and other living organisms. How can we doubt that our thoughts, not just our actions, manifest who we are?

We are more than what we see in this dimension and we are so much more than a physical being wrapped in this meat suit here on this planet to amass material wealth. Our roots are in the heavens and we need each other to complete who we are.

Whatever your religion, background, upbringing, race or heritage, all teachings from the ancient sages to modern science all point in the same direction – regardless of what we know about God and universal truth, we still want proof. Now for the first time in history science and spiritualism are on the same page. Can there be any doubt? Yes, there will always be skeptics, but to them I say keep searching, because at some point you will find your answers, if not in this material then somewhere else, and if not today then tomorrow. Remember you chose this book; it came to you for a reason, because there are no coincidences. Read it, digest it, discuss it and use it, because whatever meaning you derive, it is the meaning you were intended to receive whether you agree with this material or not there is something here you must know.

Chapter Six
Spirituality and Religion

According to the American Heritage and Webster's dictionaries, "Spirituality is having the nature of spirit; not tangible or material; concerned with or affecting the soul, perhaps pertaining to God, or belonging to a church or religion." To be sure spirituality has nothing to do with ghosts, goblins, witches, warlocks or things that go bum in the night. And you can be spiritual without believing in the existence of a God, the Light, or any other higher power.

Spirituality encompasses many disciplines, as there are countless theologies, religions, groups and organizations that practice some form of spirituality. Spirituality is about understanding nature, life, God, the Light, the Universe and the soul. It's about looking within to be a better person and to extend yourself in helping others. Spirituality comes from your heart and your soul. Spirituality does not segregate us and does not judge, justify or criticize. Spirituality is about peace, reverence, love, forgiveness and compassion.

Wikipedia states that religion is an organized approach to human spirituality which usually encompasses a set of narratives, symbols, beliefs and practices, often with a supernatural or transcendent quality, that give meaning to the practitioner's experiences of life through reference to a higher power or truth. Religion may be expressed through prayer, ritual, meditation, music and art, among other things. It may focus on specific supernatural, metaphysical, and moral claims about reality (the cosmos, and human nature), which may yield a set of religious laws, ethics, and a particular lifestyle. Religion also encompasses ancestral or cultural traditions, writings, history, and mythology, as well as personal faith and religious experience.

The term "religion" refers to both the personal practices related to communal faith and to group rituals and communication stemming from shared conviction.

"Religion" is sometimes used interchangeably with "faith" or "belief system," but it is more socially defined than personal convictions, and it entails specific behaviors.

The development of religion has taken many forms in various cultures, because it takes into account the psychological, historical and societal roots.

In Western thought, religions present a common quality, the "hallmark of patriarchal religious thought," which divides the world in two comprehensive domains, one sacred, and the other irreverent. Religion is often described as a communal system for the unity of belief focusing on a single system of thought, unseen being, person, or object, that is considered to be supernatural, sacred, divine, or of the highest truth. Moral codes, practices, values, institutions, tradition, rituals, and scriptures are often traditionally associated with core beliefs, which may overlap with concepts in secular philosophy. Religion is often described as a way of life or a stance.

Religious belief usually relates to the existence, nature and worship of a deity or deities and divine involvement in the universe and human life. Alternately, it may also relate to values and practices transmitted by a spiritual leader. Unlike other belief systems, religious belief tends to be codified in literate societies, while religion in non-literate societies is still largely passed on orally. In some religions, like the Abrahamic religions, it is held that most of the core beliefs have been divinely revealed.

Members of an organized religion may not see any significant difference between religion and spirituality. Or they may see a distinction between the routine, earthly aspects of their religion and its spiritual dimension. Some individuals draw a strong distinction between religion and spirituality. Some may see spirituality as a belief in ideas of religious significance (such as God, the Soul, or Heaven), but do not feel bound to the bureaucratic structure and creeds of a particular organized religion.

Some will choose the term spirituality rather than religion to describe their form of belief, perhaps reflecting disillusionment with organized religion, and a movement towards a more "modern" — more tolerant, and more intuitive — form of religion. These individuals may reject organized religion because of historical acts by religious organizations, such as the Christian Crusades and Islamic Jihad, or the Spanish Inquisition, which marginalized and persecuted various minorities. They may prefer a belief system with a spiritual approach to being, such as the ancient spiritual tradition of India, based on the Vedas, in which the inner reality of existence, is emphasized.

In summation, I will share with you what I have heard from hundreds of people, through discussions with them over many years. The usual consensus and differentiator between religion and spiritualism is this. Religions, although having brought together thousands and millions of people in one purpose to have a singular thought and a common sense of security and like mindedness, is viewed as having been the cause of many wars and dissension. Religion also divides us by convincing us to believe that one belief system is better than another; thus, if you don't believe as I do you are not only in opposition to me, you are against me and therefore you must be bad and perhaps you should die. Is this true for everyone? No, however many leaders of these religious organizations will, and do, cause many to rise up in arms to crush other non-believers.

Many view spiritualism as a common, non-theistic way of being, allowing acceptance of a universal power or God in which there is a place of appreciation for all to gather through love and understanding, permitting everyone the freedom of being who they choose to be, and to practice how they worship without prejudice.

I think the following from "The Daily Om" is a perfect example of how we are connected and how interdependent we are on one another for not just our survival, but for our happiness.

Picking a leaf off the ground and contemplating it as an object in and of itself is very inspiring. Its shape and color, the way it feels in your hand, its delicate veins and the stem that once held it fast to the branch of a tree—all of these qualities reveal a leaf to be a miniature work of natural art. As we contemplate this small object more deeply and consider where it came from and what purpose it has served, we find that the leaf is one small but essential part of a system that harnesses the energy of the sun, plumbs the depths of the earth, and in the process brings into being the oxygen many living things rely on to live.

A leaf transforms the elements of its environment, sunlight, carbon dioxide, and rain into nourishment for its tree. This beautiful, nearly weightless, ephemeral piece of nature is a vital conduit to the branch that is a conduit to the trunk that is a conduit to the roots of the tree. The roots, in turn, draw nourishment from the earth to feed the trunk, the branches, and the leaves. The living beings that inhale the oxygen that comes from this process exhale the carbon dioxide that feeds the leaves through which the tree is fed. It is difficult to know where one cycle ends and another one begins.

One of the many gifts that nature offers us is a clear demonstration of the interdependence between all living things. The person who exhales the carbon dioxide, the clouds that produce the rain, the sun that gives light, the leaf that transforms all these things into sustenance for a tree, not one of these could survive without being part of this cycle. Each living being is dependent upon other living things for its survival. When we look at the world, we see that this is not a place where different beings survive independently of one another. Earth is home to a web of living things that are connected to each other through a spinning kaleidoscope of relationships. We need each other to survive and thrive.

However you practice and whatever your beliefs, your mission - our mission – is to bring light into the world. So whether someone else shares your view or not we are all here for the same reason and that is to learn from one another and to, as the Beatles say so eloquently in their song of the same title, "Let it Be." But just don't let it be, let your neighbors be, stop judging and wanting to have everyone live by your rules and do things the way you think they should be done. There are few tenets to live by, the problem is it only works if we all live by them. Let's start with you and me.

Chapter Seven
The Universal Laws

Universal Laws relate to absolutely everything that you experience and create in your life. These Laws guide everything in the universe and by living in alignment with these laws; you flow with the energy of the cosmos.

Some call these Laws "Natural Laws" and some "Universal Laws" or the "Laws of Nature." Whatever you want to call them they are here for each of us to use for the benefit of all. Perhaps we shouldn't call them laws because it makes it seem like you'll go to prison if you break them. The truth is this, while there is no physical prison, unless you live within these guidelines you are already living in your own little box or prison.

The "Universal Laws" are the Law of Intention; the Law of Creation; the Law of Attraction; the Law of Allowing; the Law of Benevolence and the Law of Tithing. If we all followed these few, but simple, laws we wouldn't need any of the laws man has created. Living within these laws would help heal the planet, with each of us having the peace, love and happiness we all seek and want. By taking to understand these laws and use them we can live in harmony with nature and ourselves. All it really takes is the time to think and act with a conscience.

Laws of Science and Spirituality

These laws are actually no different in some respects than the Law of Gravity or the Laws of Physics because they all have a definitive way of working. Living within this current of energy these laws will bring you into harmony with life; a life filled with effortless manifesting, prosperity, joy, and love for every part of existence. This life energy exists because you will exist in the natural order and truths that flow throughout your soul. It is the builder of all creation.

43

Unlike man's laws with addendums and amendments these Laws do not change. They do not need to be modified, adjusted or revised. They cannot be undermined, evaded or avoided by anyone, not by the rich, not the influential, not the intellectual and not by politics or man's laws. These Laws apply to all, regardless of your race, religion, color, ethnicity, physicality, country, or level of intellect. These Laws are the same for those who know them and for those who are ignorant of them. They have existed since the beginning of time and your ignorance of them or your lack of belief in them does not invalidate them or excuse you from their power.

The Secret of the Secret

While the movie "The Secret" brought you what is known as "The Law of Attraction" it is not the only law you need to know that will provide you peace, harmony and success, it is only the beginning. Yes, since there has been so much written about the Law of Attraction and the movie The Secret, which is about the Law of Attraction it seemed like that was all that was necessary to achieving your greatest life.

While you have read about it or have seen the movie and others are just starting to experience what this is all about, it is only one source of enlightenment. First, I must tell you that whenever anyone says that this book, the one you are reading at this moment, or any other book is the only book you need to read, about these subjects, I can tell you that isn't so. Whatever you do, read everything there is about any subject you are interested in, because you never know when a work or a writer will resonate for you and you will understand the subject better and the point will hit you square between the eyes just like an arrow hits a bullseye.

I have read dozens of books on this subject and continue to read because I never know when I will receive another bit of information that will further clarify a subject or bring me new enlightenment. Life is a work in progress, there is no end, and for however long you exist in this dimension you will have something to learn.

Enlightenment

You may often question why so many people write about the same subject. It is because we all have a way of writing that will only be received by certain people; not everyone will want to buy or read that same book. Even if we all read the same book we might interpret it differently. So unless a book is deposited on your doorstep, everyone's doorstep, we will not receive the information. Even if all people received this book, still not everyone would receive the message and the message would be interpreted differently.

How many times have you read books about dieting, which literally contained the same information? However, one of the books, or chapters, or paragraphs or sentences in a one of those books stood out and all of a sudden you understood it, you used it and you lost weight. Well, why didn't you get it from the first book you read? It's a combination of things. It could be the way someone wrote it, it could be that you weren't concentrating on what you were reading, it could be the words that were written weren't quite clear, or the fact that the second book you read connected with something in the first book and you got that "aha" moment. You see you just never know when you'll get the message, even when it hits you on the head like a baseball bat. For most of us it usually takes many of the same messages and perhaps a lot of time, even years for you to get the point.

This book or the movie you recently viewed or a certain person or specific information has come into your life for a reason and it is for you to discover the reason by paying attention to it. Yet that isn't always true, is it? So perhaps this book is the one that gets your attention, that takes you on a different path, that leads you to a place where you have always wanted to go and be, that finally allows you to see your passion and a way to get there.

Shifting Your Attention

Here are some things to consider. Have you ever noticed that when you shift your attention you create a new reality? If that doesn't make sense it will. Right now, while you are reading this sentence you may or may not be fully aware of what you are reading. Our minds are always on the go. We are so easily distracted. Ever notice how many times you read the same sentence or paragraph? Perhaps you just read a whole paragraph and didn't comprehend one word? I know you have and it's like that for everyone. Not only do we not really read what we are looking at, sometimes we have a hard time comprehending it. There are all kinds of reasons for not getting the message. There's a distraction. It could be that someone walks in the room, or knocks on the door, or the phone rings and your attention shifts and you are now in another world of consciousness. It could be that your mind is wandering because you are thinking of what you want for breakfast, lunch or dinner. I know, you know what I mean.

You are creating your reality as you shift your attention. Let's say you want a new car, and that car is a new BMW. You are intent on having a new BMW and now your mind is creating ways to get that new BMW. Where you are at this moment is in the state of intention, which is you, intending on having that specific vehicle. What is the next thing you begin doing? The next thing you do is pay a lot of attention to having it. Consciously you are now attending to do everything you need to do to get that new BMW. Simply put you have placed your focus on getting that BMW so you're putting your intention out into the universe.

Conscious and Sub-Conscious Creating

This need or want you have is true for everything you have in your life from a good or bad relationship to that job or business you're in and all the money you have or lack.

Hold on a minute, am I telling you that everything you have in your life is what you want? Even the stuff you don't want? You bet it is. But I don't want to be sick and I don't want this terrible marriage or relationship and I don't want to be poor. Yes you do! Whether consciously or subconsciously you are the one creating it. This can be a rude awakening for many of us. Because it's always easier to blame your lack of anything on someone else. Unless you are making positive intentions and paying attention to those positive intentions you will get just the opposite. There's an old saying "Fail to plan and you plan to fail." What that means is that if your intention and attention don't line up, you get what shows up because you lacked focus on what you want.

Here's another example. You say, "I want to loose weight." Okay so what does it take to loose weight? Diet, exercise, how often you exercise, what exercises you do, eating smaller portions, eating less fattening foods, watch your alcohol intake, and so on and so on. So that's one part of loosing weight. Now you're saying so what else is there? Well there's how you think about how you want to look and how you really see yourself. You need to wrap your head around how you want to look. You must visualize your new self in the future. You must attend to it as if you are that person now. This is why so many people don't look like they think they want to and why so many people fail at loosing weight or having the body and health they believe they want.

Here's how my life happened even when I didn't understand the Universal Laws. In high school I was short, not that I'm tall now, but shorter. You may know of someone or have experienced what it is like to be the small kid on the block when you're growing up. You usually get picked on a lot. Well, I was singled out enough to make me upset and angry at times. So I decided that if I worked out at the gym with weights that I could make myself look like someone who you might not want to pick on. I wouldn't be so vulnerable because although I was short I would be muscular. So my intention was to look bigger and stronger and I put my intention on achieving that and I did.

I visualized how I would look and I only saw myself as how I looked, by intending to be that person and attending to being that person. I continued to do so through my years in college and in the service. It was definitely what I was intent on achieving and of course paid constant attention to my physique. Even in the service, although I didn't know of this principle, I always attained the highest physical test scores because that's what I worked on, that's what was important to me and again that's what I attended to doing and being. The best.

Consequently when I got married I shifted my attention to business, earning money and supporting a family. Not too unusual is it? I gained weight; a few inches around the waist, lost some muscle mass and became, let's just say, slightly portly. Again, it was a case of taking my intention and attention in another direction. Not that I couldn't have done both, but I took my attention away from my physique. What I focused on I got, which was better and better jobs, always making more money.

As the years go on I got divorced and I decided that I needed to look good again. This again was important to me as I saw myself as someone who needed to be fit to be attractive. Whether that was true or not, it was true for me. So now I shifted my intention to looking healthy and fit and of course put all of my attention on working out, and eating right. I went to the gym, changed my eating habits and got back the physique I had when I was younger. By the way there were no fad diets and no diet pills. We'll talk more about this later. I intended it and paid attention to it and again achieved my goal. I'm sure you get the picture.

Achieving is all about your intention and attention that gets you what you want. It's where you put all of your energy. It is that you create your intention, you place your attention on your intention and then you put your energy into where you placed your attention. Don't try to say that too fast you won't be able to talk for a week. Just to make the point one more time, it's intention, attention and energy that's gets you what you want. If these aren't present, your thoughts, feelings and actions, then the results you were looking for won't show up.

How do you think I'm writing this book? Do you know how many times I've started writing other books that never came to fruition? Do you know how many times I said tomorrow I'd begin writing? That's right, way too many to count. Those other attempts were a diversion and not a true intention.

Do you remember seeing this commercial? It starts out with the family in the kitchen preparing dinner and a voice says; broccoli $1.79, tuna $3.29, crescent rolls $2.29, getting everyone together for dinner.... Priceless! It's the same here with the Universal Laws. You can't buy them, but using them is priceless!

Now that you have some idea of how certain laws work and how much your mind has to do with everything let's talk about each law individually and see why each one is so important and how they can change your life.

Tassinello

Chapter Eight
The Law of Creation

This is about creating your world, your reality and similar to the Law of Intention as we discussed in Universal Laws. This is the first step in the creating of your intention. Sounds logical doesn't it? So why am I talking about this? While it sounds logical few people actually create what they want in their life. To reach your goal or to begin intending there must be the idea. Something you want to make and have come to fruition. You have to state what it is you want to create. It doesn't have to be something tangible. It could be I want a better relationship, I want to be healthier, I want a million dollars and so on.

The Law of Creation is doing everything in your power to formulate and visualize what you want in your life, to be who you want to be and how you want the world around you to show up. Remember failing to plan is planning to fail. So the law of creation works the same way, whether you're thinking about things you want in your life or things you don't want in your life, because it acts upon any thoughts you are having. Your thoughts have enormous power.

So now you're saying, well I have lots of thoughts, from simple things of eating, drinking, and having sex, to work, cooking and cleaning and on and on. You're right, your brain is in constant thought about meaningful and meaningless things. This is where the process starts with creating your world the way you want it to be for you and creating your world through only positive thoughts. Eliminating the chatter and all the negative things that come into your head.

Spiritual or Human Being

First you must know that you are a spiritual being having a human experience. That, in and of itself should give you enormous awareness and power in creating your world. The prerequisite for creating is in, something I spoke of earlier and that is, knowing not just believing. It is how we create and co-create everything in our lives.

We are energy and we can harness that energy whenever we want. However, we sometimes use this energy negatively without realizing it. Every year, every month, every day, every hour and every minute we are creating our life. It is in every present moment that we make our past and build our future. You may think about your past and wonder why it was the way it was and be a victim of it or you may finally realize that it is you who created your past in this very moment. At this very moment what are you doing, besides reading my book, which you will use to assist you in having what you want? At this very moment what are you doing that is creating the beautiful future that you so often envision and sometimes see in your dreams?

Our universe operates on the premise that we know we are powerful creators. The universe says that we know exactly what we want and that we know that what we are creating is what we will achieve. What the universe doesn't know is that we don't understand that we don't get that it is up to us. You believe that life is random and a matter of circumstance or chance, but it isn't. Every moment you have choices and you do choose something whether consciously or not. What you choose is obviously very critical. Because the universe is waiting for you to choose and when you do the universe says, "Your wish is my command." Just like the genie in the bottle. If you don't know how to command then you get lots of stuff you don't want.

We have people creating illness and disease without really knowing it. No one intentionally creates sickness, but that's the point. If in your mind you are not healthy, then you are not. The more thought you give to it the more it manifests itself, even subtly. You can't tell the universe, "I don't want to be poor." The universe doesn't know about, "don't want," it only hears poor. You must declare that you are rich. You must show up as rich and you are rich. In our ignorance and misunderstanding we get lots of things we don't want.

Ignorance and Watching Your Thoughts

Did you know mans laws, the laws that our legislature creates states in big bold letters "Ignorance of the law is no excuse." It is also an ancient legal doctrine. Here's the full statement:

"Ignorance of the law excuses no man; not that all men know the law; but because 'tis an excuse every man will plead, and no man can tell how to confute him." - John Selden (1584-1654) posthumously published in Table Talk, 1689.

There is another quote from Peter and Esther Fisher, "The truth is that our invisible, spiritual realm is orchestrated completely by us -- individually and collectively. Our ideas, emotions, prayers, intentions and thoughts orchestrate our lives. This is why we say, "Watch what you think, for thoughts are things!" And especially "Watch what you say, because words are also things!" This has been expanded to read this way:

"Watch your thoughts, for they become words.

Watch your words, for they become actions.

Watch your actions, for they become habits.

Watch your habits, for they become character.

Watch your character, for it becomes your destiny."

Unknown

Our thoughts, prayers and intentions assemble the invisible "particles" of the invisible spiritual realm into visible forms via a very specific "Law" - the particles are energetically assembled by our words, thoughts and emotions into things. We are the ones doing it! You are the one doing it! It is from thought that everything is created. If no one has a thought about something than it will never be created.

Leading or Being Led

Too many times we allow ourselves to be lead by others. We allow others thoughts about us, and what we should be doing, to lead to thoughts of agreement and thus we create, actually their reality, which we believe is ours and does become ours.

Look around you, from childhood to all those who have in some way influenced you in becoming who you are. Your parents, siblings, relatives, friends, teachers, books, the news, employers, the government, religious institutions and more have had an impact on your life. So good, bad or indifferent, all of your thoughts, although you thought them, have been influenced by all of these people. How many of these thoughts and the things you have in your life are actually you?

Many of you will say, "How can this be?" Do you know how the universe works scientifically? While I have explained it earlier in the Quantum Theory section we see that no one really knows exactly how the universe works. So perhaps it's a good time to shift your perspective. Perhaps I should have asked you to shift your perspective in the beginning of this book.

Shifting your perspective of course takes you away from your usual day-to-day thinking. Unfortunately you live a very rote life, a life that is usually on autopilot so to speak. You rarely create your day; it's usually one of routine. You get up at a the same time, make a cup of coffee, and listen to the news on TV or on the radio, shower, dress, perhaps have something to eat, go to work, break for lunch, back to work, home for dinner, read or watch TV, go to sleep and again and again, over and over you do the same thing. We all do this to some extent. But do you want this to be your whole life? Perhaps you do. Perhaps this is exactly the way you want your life to be. So you need to ask yourself if you want a break from the routine, so you actually create your life and take responsibility for it? Or will the rest of your life be at the mercy of someone else so you can say they did it to me. It's always easier to blame someone else than to take responsibility, isn't it?

Once there was a disciple of a Greek philosopher who was commanded by his Master to give money to everyone who insulted him for three years. When this trial period was over the Master said to him, "Now you can go to Athens to learn Wisdom." When the disciple was entering Athens he met a certain wise man who sat at the gate insulting everyone who came and went. He also insulted the disciple who burst out laughing. "Why do you laugh when I insult you said the wise man?" "Because," said the disciple, "for three years I have been paying for this kind of thing and now you give it to me for nothing." "Enter the city," said the wise man, "it is all yours...."

Creating You

As I am writing this, another thought crossed my mind that may help you look at life with a new positive perspective to help you see and understand and to help you create your new life starting now.

Like you and of course like many of you, you pick a direction and continue in that direction sometimes in spite of signs and signals that say, "Hey you need to change course, you're headed in the wrong direction." You become so focused on an outcome that may not really serve you just because you don't want to begin again. I am very focused on writing and completing this book because I know that the information will help many of you to see differently, and perhaps look at things from another perspective. Whether that means seeing you, others, or the world with new eyes or how to find the passion in you to move mountains. It could be to be someone new or to create the best new thing-a-ma-gig that improves the world. Yet with all of my focus on writing I still discover new things, new people and new perspectives.

Take this Perspective

I subscribe to emails and information from many people and companies. Well yesterday I received an email from TED.com. TED stands for Technology, Entertainment, and Design. It is a diverse community of curious souls, as TED depicts itself, who can engage each other to discuss and share new ideas that can change attitudes, lives and ultimately, the world. The talk I listened to and read about was from Aimee Mullins.

Now many would say Aimee Mullins has a disability because Aimee Mullins was born without fibular bones. She had both of her legs amputated below the knee when she was an infant. But Aimee doesn't see herself as disabled, in fact she sees herself as gifted. Aimee Mullins was a record-breaker at the Paralympic Games in 1996. She has also built a career as a model, actor and activist for women, in sports and in the next generation of prosthetics.

How could Aimee do this? While I can't speak for Aimee, I can guess that Aimee had a passion to do something very specific with her life. Something that many of us only dream of doing and never does. She had a passion to be who she saw herself to be and created the Aimee Mullins she saw through intention and attention. She learned to not only walk on prosthetics, but to run on them and win medals. Aimee was so creative that she had 12 pairs of prosthetic legs created for her. She had them made for a different look and for a different outcome. She even has one pair that made her taller, over 6 ft tall in fact.

One evening she was meeting a friend at a bar and as she entered her friend saw her and commented, "That's not fair you are so tall." Well then what is fair? Of course she was joking, however you can see that although many would say Aimee has a disability, she, in fact, has greater abilities than many.

So who is to say what is fair and what is not? It's actually all about perspective, opening up your senses, seeking new realities, creating a new world through intention and yes attention.

Are you starting to get the picture or are you still in denial or disbelief that you can change your life, your circumstances, and your destiny. Do you still feel controlled or unable to make changes because of your circumstances? Or is it time to change your perspective, to change you, to do everything you have wanted to do?

Your Relationships

If you want to create better relationships, then first take a look at the relationships you have. The terrible boss, the unpleasant friend, the difficult marriage or relationship, perhaps an overbearing parent or sibling and so on. Now when you look at these relationships, what do they have in common? It's you, isn't it? So does that mean you're the problem? Not necessarily, it just means that you had a hand in creating it. One of the most difficult things to admit is the fact that we are part of the equation in a bad relationship.

How do you fix them? As Gandhi said, "You must be the change you wish to see in the world." Fortunately you can change what you do, how you act and how you perceive someone else's actions. Unfortunately, you can't change them. While I can't fix your relationships or give you advice about each of them, I can tell you that you are always in control of the outcome. It may not be easy or quick or without difficulty, but you have the power and the ability to make any relationship better. Look at your actions and make the changes necessary to heal them. Perhaps all it takes is to change your perception, act out of love or not react each time your button gets pushed. Of course I must ask you, "Why are you wearing that "Button" to begin with?"

None of us likes to admit or believe that we could be part of the problem, but we are. Sorry, there I said it again. You're gonna have to get used to it. Now you can do the "but" thing all day long, and it won't change those situations. They're in the past all you can do is move forward and learn from those experiences.

Let me give you an example of how we refuse to take responsibility for our actions. If you have ever been to traffic school and don't tell me you've never been to traffic school. I can't speak for other countries but almost everyone in the

US has been to traffic school. Just in case you haven't been there, here's what happens in the beginning of the class. The instructor asks each person to state why he or she is there. Now it's a simple question, just answer it with something like I was speeding or I drove through a red light or a stop sign, or whatever it is that you did. However, some people have to tell their story of how they were innocent (perhaps they were, but most aren't) or they had an out-of-body experience. Something took control of them.

Here's how their story goes. Well, it was about 2 am in the morning and there wasn't anyone around (except for the cop) and I slowed down for the stop sign and I looked both ways and there weren't any cars in sight so I saw it was safe to proceed. I explained that to the officer, so he shouldn't have given me a ticket. As if 2 am meant that the stop sign need not be obeyed. This is a simple example of not owning up to their part in creating this situation.

Again while this is a very simple analogy it just points to the fact that we just don't like to own that we can be a part of a problem. It's typically always someone else doing something to us.

You make excuses all the time and you do it at work, at play and in relationships. Are you perfect? Well in a sense you are, you just don't always act perfectly. When someone questions what you are doing at work or how a project is coming along you become defensive. If your spouse asks you about something you were supposed to do, you don't typically give a straight answer do you? You again become defensive. It's like you're saying, "How dare anyone question me." When you fail to be a team player, to act in the best interests of everyone, you become defensive. Typically you are on the defense, because you don't want to be seen, or feel, like you did something wrong. But this is all in our head, you can't know what someone is thinking or even what they meant most times. Then again if you are the one asking these questions how did you come across?

Smile, the universe is telling you that it will be all right if you try and you take responsibility for your actions. Rise above the din, be calm and centered and take deep breaths. I know you can do this.

Are You Acting or Re-Acting?

Reacting takes you away from acting consciously and it takes you out of thinking mode. Even though you may believe that you know someone and how they act, step back try and take a new perspective and a new way of being. Can you act and not react?

So may times you are at odds, not with someone else, but with yourself. You don't like the fact that someone said something about what you were doing. You instantly put on this suit of armor, as a shield from what you think is an attack on you. If you act and not react, it means that you took the time to think about what you were going to do.

Reaction is an automatic response that comes from fear. Well, you can say fear of what? It is the fear of so many little things that we are not even aware of most times. Even if you felt you did something correctly, many times when someone questions you, you became fearful that you may have done something wrong and you react negatively. Instead of digesting the comment or question and thinking about a reply we become defensive. Most questions are very innocent, and just that, a question of inquiry, which has no other meaning.

Conversely, the other side of that coin is this. Do you, as the questioner, take a moment to phrase your question properly so it is not offensive? This is what I mean by "we are co-creators of our reality." You must think before you act in questioning and answering. You can be the change of every relationship.

When we speak of the Law of Creation it's not just about what you will create for yourself in who you want to be, but also in whom you will be with others and how you will show up in this life. Be introspective, really search within and find your true loving spirit and act for yourself and act with love, compassion and thoughtfulness.

Responsibility

Are you the same person in your business life as you are in your personal life? I think many of us look at a business as an entity all by itself, as if it had a life of its own, as if a business could run itself without human intervention. It is also interesting that many people who manage these companies mistakenly believe that corporate responsibility has little to do with personal responsibility.

Ever wonder why companies make products or do things that don't serve the interests of the people or the planet? How is it that the employees believe that the waste or products they are creating will not affect them or their families? It's really absurd to think that you are out of harms way. Just because the by-products or waste a company creates doesn't end up directly in your backyard, or does it, doesn't mean you will be immune to its destructive nature. Somehow those pollutants end up in the ocean or the lakes or the air where you play, live or work and you become a victim of that waste. If you are aware that what you are doing is not for the greater good, that it will negatively affect someone else, if even it were possible that you could avoid its negative affects how can you in good conscience sleep at night and feel good about yourself?

Now, thankfully, there are companies that do act with a conscience not just with the products that they make, and how they treat the waste, but also in how they respect their employees. These companies show that they really care and you can find many of them listed in Fortune 500 magazine. These companies understand that they too live in the same world where they work. They care about their products, the proper disposal of its waste and they care about their employees. They don't have to think about the past, because they are creating the best of everything in the present. And they don't have to worry about defending themselves because they act with a conscience, which makes their future and our future very bright.

Chapter Nine
The Law of Intention

Intention is a determination to act in a certain way or to perform an action with a specific purpose. Whether an action is successful or unsuccessful depends at least on whether the intended result was brought about by an act or instance of determining mentally upon some action or result. So it is our thoughts that create the idea and our thoughts that allow us the intention to carry out our creation.

The Law of Intention is based on the fact that the universe has an infinite amount of energy for you to create whatever you want. One of the fallacies of our thinking and what many believe is that there is lack in our world. In other words we have been taught that there is a finite amount of resources. It's almost as if the world were flat and you would eventually sail off the edge, or that there was only enough energy and resources in the universe to manufacture 100 million cars or 100 million homes or 100 million computers. Does anyone really believe that we can't create enough to fill our demand for these things? While we can speculate that we will run out of specific resources may be true, we have and will continue to have the power to find other resources and other ways of creating what we need.

Once we truly understand that everything is energy and there is an infinite amount of energy we can then understand and manage the ability to create anything we want. Creating what you want does not deprive someone or anyone else from having what they want. Your wanting and getting does not create a lack for someone else so you can stop hoarding. All hoarding does is increase the cost of that resource and creates an artificial lack.

Your Thoughts

Everything begins in our mind with our thoughts. Our thoughts are what make you who you are. It's what drives you to do things, good, bad or indifferent. Can you name anything you can do without the function of our mind?   Mind boggling, isn't it? I know you know this, but sometimes you have to say it to really get it.

Ever notice that when you say something to yourself, that is to think it and not say it out loud, it resonates and manifests itself a specific way as opposed to when you say it out loud to someone else or even yourself? Speaking the words allows them to resonate differently and it can take on a whole new meaning. Also by saying it to someone else gives it more power, your intention grows, you pay more attention to it and like magic it appears. It has a different energy about it, and since it is energy it vibrates at a frequency to become manifest.

Manifest Destiny

Here's a concept of how we are influenced and how we can have things come into being, which is called "Manifest Destiny." Many history buffs know of this concept.

Manifest Destiny heavily influenced American policy in the 1800s. The idea was the driving force behind the rapid expansion of America into the West from the East, and it was heavily promoted in newspapers, posters, and through other mediums. While Manifest Destiny was not itself an official government policy, it led to the passage of legislation such as the Homestead Act, which encouraged Westward colonization and territorial acquisition. It also played an important role in American thought.

John O'Sullivan, an American newspaper editor who was writing about the proposed annexation of Texas, first used the term Manifest Destiny in 1845. He stated that it was America's "Manifest Destiny" to overspread the continent. The editorial suggested that through expansion, the United States could become a recognized political and social superpower. America had, in fact, O'Sullivan argued, been uniquely chosen for the task of expanding westward, driving out the wilderness and establishing civilization.

The Westward expansion of the United States did not, of course, begin with Manifest Destiny. The Louisiana Purchase of 1803, in which 23% of the existing territory of the United States was acquired, was probably the first major step. The government saw the appeal in acquiring more land, as well as the potential political power, which large tracts of land could confer upon the young nation. As a result, a policy pursuing aggressive expansion was actively pursued. The idea of Manifest Destiny was merely a component, and one, which captured the popular imagination.

O'Sullivan's editorial added fuel to the fire with a catchy phrase. Numerous government campaigns painted the allures of the West for prospective settlers, and promoted programs, which could help people, acquire and hold land in the West. With the discovery of gold and other valuable minerals, a tide of Easterners started to pour into the West, supported by their belief in their right and duty to expand.

The idea of Manifest Destiny was also behind American political actions overseas. Although the term ceased to be used in a political context in the early twentieth century, the far-reaching impact of it was clear. A section of the editorial reminded Americans that they were uniquely positioned to spread democracy throughout the world, and this concept clearly played a role in twentieth century American foreign policy. Many historians use the term "Manifest Destiny" to refer to the period in American history which was marked by rapid expansion "from sea to shining sea" through annexation of the Western half of the continent.

Manifest Destiny was a concept or a creation and from that creation came intention and from that intention people paid attention to it and so it became real. Yes, you do manifest your own destiny, so why not manifest exactly what you want?

Butterflies and Apple Seeds

Have you ever heard of the butterfly principle? It goes like this, "a butterfly, flapping its wings in Japan effects the rainfall in Seattle." No? That's because I just made up that one. The actual saying by Edward Lorenz is "A butterfly, flapping its wings in one part of the world, could affect the weather on the other side of the globe." May sound silly, however it is true because whenever there is any action, no matter how minute, it generates motion and energy, which touches and affects everything and all of us.

Everything in the universe is energy and you and I can use this energy for the good of ourselves. As we know, what you intend is what you will go about doing and that intention is built into the fabric of life. It is everything from a blade of grass to a tree to all animal and human life and I do mean everything.

Let's consider minor things such as an apple seed. Do you believe that an apple seed has an intention? Well it must have intention or it wouldn't become an apple tree and have more apples with seeds. The intention of these plants never waivers, they become what they are intent on becoming. An acorn becomes an oak tree; a seed of grass becomes your lawn, and so on as it is for every living thing. All DNA has intention built into it.

Quirky Quarks and More

To understand this concept a little better, although I will use definitions and explanations from Wikipedia, we need to go deeper into particles and subatomic particles to what we know as the smallest piece of all these particles. A subatomic particle is an elementary or composite particle smaller than an atom. Particle physics and nuclear physics are concerned with the study of these particles, their interactions, and non-atomic matter.

Subatomic particles include the atomic constituents electrons, protons, and neutrons. Protons and neutrons are composite particles, consisting of quarks. A proton contains two up quarks and one down quark, while a neutron consists of one up quark and two down quarks and the quarks are held together in the nucleus by gluons.

There are six different types of quark in all ('up', 'down', 'bottom', 'top', 'strange', and 'charm'), as well as other particles including photons and neutrinos, which are produced copiously in the sun. Most of the particles that have been discovered are encountered in cosmic rays interacting with matter and are produced by scattering processes in particle accelerators. There are dozens of known subatomic particles.

In particle physics, the conceptual idea of a particle is one of several concepts inherited from classical physics, the world we experience, that are used to describe how matter and energy behave at the molecular scales of quantum mechanics. As physicists use the term, the meaning of the word "particle" is one, which understands how particles are radically different at the quantum-level and rather different from the common understanding of the term.

The idea of a particle is one, which had to undergo serious rethinking in light of experiments, which showed that the smallest particles (of light) could behave just like waves. The difference is indeed vast, and required the new concept of wave-particle duality to state that quantum-scale "particles" are understood to behave in a way, which resembles both particles and waves.

Another new concept, the uncertainty principle, meant that analyzing particles at these scales required a statistical approach. All of these factors combined so that the very notion of a discrete "particle" has been ultimately replaced by the concept of something like wave-packet of an uncertain boundary whose properties are only known as probabilities, and whose interactions with other "particles" remains largely a mystery, even 80 years after quantum mechanics was established.

From Einstein's hypotheses and studies energy and matter are analogous: matter can be thoroughly denoted in terms of energy. Thus, we have only discovered two mechanisms in which energy can be transferred. These are particles and waves. For example, light can be expressed as both particles and waves. This paradox is known as the Duality Paradox.

Through the work of Albert Einstein, Louis de Broglie, and many others, current scientific theory holds that all particles also have a wave nature. This phenomenon has been verified not only for elementary particles, but also for compound particles like atoms and even molecules. In fact, according to traditional formulations of non-relativistic quantum mechanics, wave–particle duality applies to all objects, even macroscopic ones.

Let's Talk DNA and Intention

As we know everything is energy just vibrating at a different frequency and the fabric of the universe and every living thing has intention built into it. So this means that all DNA, our DNA as we know it is energy and has intention.

As an example, when sperm is injected into an egg it combines with the egg to form that from which it was produced, whether it's from an animal or man. The sperm from your father combined with the egg from your mother has intention built into it. From conception it knows what it will be. It knows how you will develop: how tall you will be, what will be the shape of your features, whether more from your father's side or more from your mother's side. It knows how long you will live, barring some accident. It knows the color of your hair and your eyes and your skin color and so much more. It knows everything at that moment of conception of who you will be physically and more.

So when we talk about intention, it is what you will do and how you will show up for yourself and the world. If you lack intention or fail to make a decision to do whatever your subconscious or conscious mind has thought of, it is the same as allowing someone else to make your decisions for you and have no intention at all. That's right it's the same as the example I provided before. "Failing to plan is the same as planning to fail." Unless you decide, unless you intend and attend to manifest something, what will come to fruition is something you may not want. You must do something, you cannot sit on a rock thinking of having something and believing it will happen without a physical action on your part.

So many of us sit around and ponder what we will do in our lives. How will I find a good mate? How will I find a good job or build my own business? How will I have an athletic body? Whatever your goal if you just think about it and continue with doubts about it you will not achieve it.

Saying things like "you know I'm going to try out this new diet and see how it goes," has no intention of happening. There is no intention to actually pay attention to it and make it work. You have not made the decision to have it be successful because you have not made the commitment to make it so.

Trying is only that, it is a wishy-washy ploy to deceive yourself into believing you may actually achieve your goal. While you believe you will achieve your goal, it's not a real goal, because you are not really intent on reaching it.

You will allow excuses to creep in. I just couldn't eat what I was supposed to everyday because; I just couldn't get to the gym because; I just couldn't get that thesis completed I was too tired. I just couldn't, just goes on and on doesn't it? It's not, I just couldn't, it's I'm just not really willing to do what it takes to reach my goal. It's either not a real goal or you're not willing to stretch yourself, to go the distance or to do what it takes to make it happen. Other excuses like, "I don't have the time," means I'm not willing to make the time to do that. You and I have the same amount of time in each day, so what are you wanting and willing to do with that time?

Sometimes you really believe that you are doing your best, but if you look at the results, or lack thereof, you'd have to admit that you really weren't intent on reaching your goal or hitting your target. Because everything you really want you have.

Being Honest

When I was managing a sales team we all had goals. In setting goals you needed a target whether it was a specific type of business or industry, size, location, number of employees or any information that would make them a potential customer. While there are many conditions to be met, all sales become a numbers game. Additionally, you had to understand your closing ratio; looking at how many potential prospects you need to make a sale. As an example in the telecommunications business we needed 20 potential prospects, which in turn would yield 5 qualified prospects, which would yield 2 sales on average. Knowing this provides the big target.

This is where being honest, not just with your manager, but more importantly with yourself comes into play. While you know you need 20 potential customers to reach the average of 2 sales, you actually need a target list of let's say 50. The easy way out is to make a big target list of unqualified prospects. This is how you typically delude yourself into believing something that probably isn't true because you don't properly qualify the potential target and because you don't want to do the additional work necessary.

You're really not honest with yourself as to what it will take to reach your goal because it may take more work than you are ready for or want to do. So while you really know what to do, unless you are absolutely intent on making it happen, you will not. Unless you are honest enough with yourself about what is happening you will fall short. And when it becomes too late, you will make all kinds of excuses to yourself and others because you can't be wrong or take the responsibility for your own actions. Finally you'll blame it on the customer, or the system or the company.

You can see how necessary it is to be honest with yourself so you're intention and attention line up to reach your goals. Believing that you are doing your best and knowing you are doing your best are two distinct paths. Like you, I have had so many ideas about what I want to be and do in my life and I have failed at many of them because these thoughts were just that, a thought, which wasn't carried through with an intention. I really wasn't intent on making it happen. I wasn't committed to realizing that idea. It was more like making busy work so you convince yourself that you're doing something productive when you're not.

Believing and Knowing – There is a Difference

Here's the difference between believing and knowing. If you placed a marble on a slanted table do you believe it will hit the floor or do you know it will hit the floor? Of course you know it will hit the floor, because you know the effects of gravity and you have experienced it before. So if you want to know that you will do something you must stop believing something will happen and know it will happen not just by your intention, but also by your attention to it. Know you will do it and you will. Believe you will do it and perhaps it will be done. Do you want to take that chance? Perhaps the odds in Las Vegas will change too.

There are times in life when we are committed to pursuing our passions. Every molecule in our body is focused on doing what we love. At other times, necessity and responsibility dictate that we put our dreams aside and do what needs to be done. It is during these moments that we may choose to forget what it is that we love to do. There is any number of reasons for why we may leave our passions behind.

A hobby may lose its appeal once we realize it will never turn into our dream job. Someone important to us may keep telling us that our passions are childish and unrealistic, until we finally believe them. Forgetting about what you love to do can be a form of self-sabotage. If you can forget about your dreams, then you never have to risk failure. Just because we've decided to ignore our passions doesn't mean they no longer exist.

Nothing can fill the emptiness that remains in a space vacated by a passion that we have tossed aside. Besides, life is too short to stop doing what you love, and it is never too late to rediscover your favorite things. If you gave up playing an instrument, painting, drawing, spending time in nature, or any other activity or interest that you once loved to do, now may be the time to take up that passion again. If you don't remember what it is that you used to be passionate about, you may want to think about the activities or interests that you used to love or the dreams that you always wished you could pursue.

You don't have to neglect your responsibilities to pursue your passions, and you don't have to neglect your commitments to do what you love. When you make an effort to incorporate your interests into your life, the fire within you ignites. You feel excited, inspired, and are fed by the flames that are sparked by living your life with passion for what you love.

Your Greater Power Within

This quote from Steve Pavlina from his Cause-effect vs. Intention-Manifestation is another example of how intention works. "You might assume that the cause of an effect would be a series of physical and mental actions leading up to that effect. Action-reaction. If your goal is to make dinner, then you might think the cause would be the series of preparation steps.

"To an outside observer, that certainly appears to be the case. The scientific method would suggest that this is how things work, based on a purely objective observation.

"However, within your own consciousness, you know that the series of action steps is not the real cause. The actions are themselves an effect, aren't they?

"What's the real cause? The real cause is the decision you made to create that effect in the first place. That's the moment you said to yourself, "let it be" or "make it so." At some point you decided to make dinner. That decision may have been subconscious, but it was still a decision. Without that decision the dinner would never manifest. That decision ultimately caused the whole series of actions and finally the manifestation of your dinner.

"From where does that decision arise? It might arise from your subconscious, or in the case of conscious decisions, it arises from your consciousness. Ultimately your consciousness is the greater power, as it can override subconscious choices once it becomes aware of them."

Missing this very simple distinction has contributed to quite a number of failed goals. Let me give you an example of expectation of intention and why your intention must totally be based on expectation.

I just completed a coaching call with a client where we were discussing his business and how to get more clients. As he was describing what he was doing, he mentioned that he had to have 1000 people in his database before he would begin his e-mail campaign. I asked why he needed 1000 before he began the campaign. He said, "That according to some books I read on marketing and from some previous experiences the return rate on marketing is 1%," meaning that for every 100 people you contact you will get 1 person as a client. So I asked again, "Why do you need 1000 to begin your campaign," and he said, "Because I need 10 clients." So why not begin the email campaign with 500 now, why wait?

Even more than this simple strategy is why not expect a different result? Why not make your intention to have 20 clients by emailing to a database of 1000? Here's why we get stuck. For intention to work you need to get out of the box you're in, the box you created that says I can only expect "x" because this is what I have been told or because of my last or previous experience. Change your expectation, change your intention and don't just believe they will manifest themselves, know they will manifest themselves.

This is a very important distinction. Remove yourself from your limiting beliefs, either because you were told what to expect or because you had a previous similar experience. As they say, "If you continue to do the same thing over and over again, don't expect a different result." Or are you satisfied with the results you're getting?

So as a result of this conversation he got the message about expectation and intention. You must go outside of your box, expand or redefine your expectation and know that what you intend will become your manifestation.

Coincidence or Providence?

So why is this book in your hands today? While I am in the middle of writing this book, I know that you are reading it because I am intent on not just completing it but having it read by millions. It is a complete focus to manifest my dream from my subconscious into a conscious decision to not let anything stop me.

Here's the other part of that decision and that is completing the work. What is my intention of when will it be done? As with the example of sales prospects earlier it is the same here. How many pages are typically necessary? Well, there could be 20 pages or 500 pages. So I'm guessing that I have more than enough material for a few hundred pages and my intention is to write at least 150. Great, so how many pages can I write in a day? Let's say 5 pages a day. That means that it will take (150 divided by 5) 30 days. I have a clear and manageable goal. I know exactly what I have to do to manifest the writing of this book.

Now comes the really hard part and that is actually doing the work. Will I stick to my goal and not let anything interfere with it or will I use every excuse imaginable to not complete what I set out to do? By the way I came back to this sentence to let you know that from the thought of writing this, through writing, editing and to publishing took 6 months.

I know right now you're ready to make those commitments and that's great, but don't miss the rest of the ingredients necessary to be everything you intend on being and have all the happiness you want and deserve and have the same for the rest of the world.

Right now I want you to declare to yourself, and to the universe, who and what you are. Do not ask to be so and so, or ask to have such and such. Declare that you have it now and you will have it because you have just marshaled all the forces of the universe to assist you in achieving your goals, the universe is on your side. Also what you are declaring for yourself cannot be at the expense of someone else.

To get you started I want you to get a notepad and make 2 columns. On that pad in the left column I want you to declare who you are or what you want in your life. Then in the right column I want you to write your intention about what you will do to get or have it.

(Here are some examples)

<u>You</u>	<u>Intention</u>
<u>Are a good person</u>	<u>Smile, laugh and be happy</u>
<u>Are starting a new co.</u>	<u>Envision your company</u>
<u>Are a writer</u>	<u>See yourself writing</u>
<u>Are creative</u>	<u>Visualize your completed project</u>
<u>Have a new mate</u>	<u>See every detail of that person</u>

In this next section I want you to declare your capabilities (examples)

<u>I know how to build a business plan</u>

<u>I am a great writer, or actor, or farmer or business person</u>

<u>I know how to make furniture, or ski, or sing</u>

<u>I'm a great cook and I have lots of recipes</u>

<u>I'm very athletic and can run a mile in 4 minutes</u>

<u>I know how to manage a business</u>

Tassinello

Keep at this until you discover your passion. Then set your intention to see it through. I would say I wish you good luck, but luck has nothing to do with this. It is all in your intention and then paying attention to it.

Chapter Ten
The Law of Attraction

The Law of Attraction is certainly a hot topic. How can I top what has already been written about this subject? Well maybe I can't and maybe I can, but seriously it's not about being better than someone else, it's about adding to the collective and enhancing what has already been written.

If you haven't heard of the Law of Attraction this will be very enlightening, if you have and if you've tried it and it hasn't worked the way you thought it might, this will help you. Why it probably didn't work well is because the Universal Laws work as a collection. In other words you have to use all of them to get the results you want. It's like having a car with no engine or tires or steering wheel. If you don't have all parts the car isn't going to take you anywhere.

This is why I began with the Law of Creation and then the Law of Intention. If I have no ideas, or an idea, of what I want to create then I can't intend it and of course can't attract it. Then again my thoughts are always creating something so if I don't control those thoughts then I get lots of stuff I don't want.

Regardless, of which comes first or second, this information is to make you aware of all the Laws that are working within the universe, which in spite of your ignorance of them, are operating all the time. There is not a time when they rest. Whether I have the correct order of these Laws or not makes no difference as they all apply all the time.

So what came first the chicken or the egg? Guess we can debate that for an hour or two. Since I am here, and I have thought, I believe my first thought is about creating something I want or I think I need.

Tassinello

Do You Really Need It?

Let's define want and need. A need is something you have to have, something you can't do without. A good example is food. If you don't eat, you won't survive for long. Many people have gone days without eating, but they eventually had to eat to survive. You might not need a whole lot of food, but you do need to eat.

A want is something you would like to have. It is not absolutely necessary, but it would be a good thing to have. A good example is music. Now, some people might argue that music is a need because they think they can't do without it. But you don't need music to survive. You do need to eat.

On the other hand these are general categories, of course. Some categories have both needs and wants. For instance, food could be a need or a want, depending on the type of food you want to eat, however if it's food or no food then you will take what you can get for survival.

So you have thoughts about these things every minute and every day. You bring them into existence every minute of every day. Sometimes you get what you want and sometimes you don't. So why don't you get what you want all the time? Because you get the things you don't want when you are thinking "I don't want such and such." The laws are always working and listening to your thoughts. The universe says I will give you what you are thinking about. So if you're thinking about things you don't want, you will manifest them because the universe doesn't recognize, "I don't" or "No" or any negative word. It only knows that you are thinking about "X" and "X" and this is what you will receive. Confusing? Unsettling? Yes, I understand.

Understanding and Power

You must understand the absolute power of these Laws and the relationship between your thoughts and feelings and what you will manifest in your life. I can look at what I have manifested in my life right now and I can see how I came to be where I am today. I can ask, "Why am I divorced?" I can ask, "Why am I lacking money?" The fact is I know why I am where I am because I created, intended and attracted this so I could have the time to study, understand and write. And while I'm doing this I am manifesting the resources to have all of this come to fruition. It's not that it may happen, IT IS HAPPENING NOW!

Some of you are asking, "Arthur, why did you make it so difficult?" I 'm glad I asked myself this question for you. My answer is this. I needed to let go of my ego and learn what real humility is about. It didn't have anything to do with my being a bad person or not knowing how to give material things or myself. For me it was more about my attachment to material things and my truly understanding what I thought was lacking in my life. My life is the way it is because I intended it to come full circle in understanding what I am writing about and to manifest all the information I have received to fully comprehend my time on this planet. This manifestation in my life, as difficult as it looks and incongruous as it may seem, was necessary for me to find the real Arthur and to recognize my spirit and know how deeply my love is of you and me and God.

Could I have written this while I was running my other business? Perhaps I could, because I have multitasked several businesses at once before, but my other business was disconnected from what I have chosen as the next and final chapter of my life.

Although many people know me and saw me as kind or generous or smart or giving or spiritual, I didn't always see this in myself. I didn't feel I was all I could be and who I was meant to be in this lifetime. Right now, even if this book only reached a few, I would have spoken the truth and empowered others to know that wealth is not just about money. Don't misunderstand me, money is good if you allow it for good, but real wealth is about well-being. And that is giving and receiving well-being. Will I make money from what I write? Yes, I will, and I will use it in much better ways today than if I had received it before this day.

We are all so much more than who we believe we are in this physical body. This meat suit, so to speak, that we wear each day, this meat suit that houses our spirit. If I were to remove you and everyone else from this shell, this meat suit, you and I would look the same. Then how would we judge one another? We wouldn't and that's the point. Judging another has no value, as it only serves to separate us. Observing and learning from another does have value.

The Physical vs. The Spiritual

Let's look at it this way. Right now your outer being is thinking about how you did a great job of painting a room. Your inner being is looking at that same handy work and saying, "You know it really isn't that great you missed a few spots." There is this disconnect from your outer being, the physical painter, and your inner being, the spiritual you, that just told you what you didn't want to admit and created a negative emotion within you. On the other hand when you do great things outwardly and your inner being feels that you did do a great job, you then get a positive emotion. It is your "gut", your "source" or as the Kahuna says, your "naau" always knows the truth and tells you so.

You cannot escape the truth of who you are or what you have done or how you show up. These vibrations are responsible for your management. So reinvent who you are and be all you can be.

Speaking of reinventing, let's look at one of the oldest inventions: the common wheel. The wheel goes back to the Stone Age, yet that hasn't stopped thousands of people from reinventing the wheel. Reminds me of the saying, "you don't have to reinvent the wheel." Perhaps the wheel does need reinventing and of course it has been reinvented several times, thank goodness. Most things that have been invented are improved upon, or enhanced. Perhaps it's time for you to reinvent something if that's what you need to do and use your intention and attention to begin the process. Perhaps it's time to reinvent you?

Shifting Perspective

So you may ask, "What does shifting perspective have to do with the Law of Attraction?" You always ask such great questions. Here is a story from the Dalai Lama.

"The ability to shift perspective can be one of the most powerful and effective tools we have to help us cope with life's daily problems. The ability to look at events from different perspectives can be very helpful then, practicing this, one can use certain experiences, certain tragedies to develop a calmness of mind. One must realize that every phenomena, every event, has different aspects. Everything is of a relative nature.

"It often seems that when problems arise, our outlook becomes narrow. All of our attention becomes focused on worrying about the problem, and we may have a sense that we're the only one going through such difficulty. This can lead to a kind of self-absorption that can make the problem seem very intense. When this happens, I think that seeing things from a wider perspective can definitely help realizing, for instance that there are many other people who have gone through similar experiences. This practice of shifting perspective can even be helpful in certain illnesses or when in pain. At the time the pain arises it is of course very difficult, at that moment, to do formal meditation practices to calm the mind. But if you can make comparisons, view your situation from a different perspective, somehow something happens. If you look only at that one event, then it appears bigger and bigger. If you focus too closely, too intensely, on a problem when it occurs, it appears uncontrollable. But if you compare that event with some other great event, look at the problem from a distance, then it appears smaller and less overwhelming."

In essence what the Dalai Lama is saying is that where you place your attention is what you will receive. By changing how you look at a problem, by changing your perspective, by not making it something overwhelming, by focusing on the good things in your life and what you really want to do and where you want to take your life your attention will then eliminate the seemingly overwhelming problem and bring you that which you really want. Peace of mind.

Let's use a different example of how perspective and changing your attention will facilitate your having better experiences in your life. Mostly we like to talk about how you will manifest money into your life, but money is really only one little bit of your life. Money can only buy you material things.

Suppose you have a disagreement with someone you have known for years and you disagree so vehemently it makes you very angry. Obviously, your getting angry does nothing in coming to some understanding. It may make the other person upset and certainly makes you upset and ill and does nothing to change the other person.

While we can't change someone else we can change our point of view and perhaps agreeing to disagree will allow each of you to look at the other persons perspective. We all have positive and negative tendencies and qualities. No one is totally wrong or totally right. It is only to a degree and what serves each of you the best.

You can look at this situation from a distance and try to understand what it was in the conversation that got you so upset. No matter how intense the conversation, you must realize that this person, who you usually like didn't mean to harm you; they just had a different perspective.

Of course trying to monitor your every thought is not possible. But monitoring those major thoughts, especially the ones that will give rise to words is the answer to manifesting what you want or how you act. In addition it is those feelings of your inner being that will tell you if you are on the correct path. Every one of us knows when we are acting out of kindness, goodness and integrity. While you may be an actor at times, you cannot manipulate or make-up who you are spiritually. Happiness for yourself and others comes from honesty and compassion.

It's All Up to You

The Law of Attraction isn't necessarily an instant manifestation and it's not magic. As we said earlier you attract what you have into your life whether you believe you asked for it or not. As you think and act so the universe follows your lead. If you awake in a good mood and smile, the day usually follows along. And certainly this is a very good way to start your day and continue to do this throughout the day because the alternative should not be acceptable.

Being happy and positive is all up to you. You get to choose how to be every day with everything. If your boss comes up to you and isn't very friendly when he asks you about a project, you can decide how you want to reply and make it a positive meeting, or can meet him at his level and have a not so nice encounter. You are a part of the equation and you are a co-creator. Now if it happens that you decide to meet him at his level, will you turn around later and say bad things about your boss?

I'll probably say this a few more times, "You must be the change you wish to see in the world." If you don't change then the outcome will always be the same. Or put another way, "Doing the same things over and over again and expecting a different result is a form of insanity."

Let's talk about the speed at which you can manifest something. You know when I decided to begin writing I thought about the time frame in which I could complete this book and set a realistic goal with a little bit of stretching myself. However, I realized that because I was so passionate about what I was doing that the more I wrote and as the volume grew and the words flowed, I wrote more and more each day. I was excited, not only that I actually got started, but also I could see the light at the end of the tunnel, and it wasn't an oncoming train.

Listening to Your Inner Self

This is the way the universe works and helps you. The more attention you give to something the faster it will manifest itself. You can say well, of course you're working on it day and night. Not really. I'm paying attention to my inner being that tells me when to work long hours and when to take time for myself. Part of the difference is that the universe is providing me with the ability and the words to continue on. I'm not stuck in what to write next and again it's my intention, attention and passion that will provide a successful outcome.

I went from a thought about creating a book, to intending it to happen, to having the universe help me attract it and it showing up because the universe is responding to my positively charged vibration. It directs me and gives me the words to write, it tells me which book to pick up and where to go to get ideas for a section or a sentence or a paragraph. The way I see writing is that it is just like having a conversation with you. It's as if I we were sitting across from you answering your questions. Right now the reason I am talking about writing is because I know that many of you have a lot of interesting things to say that many of us want to hear and this may give you the impetus to begin your own book.

Lessons

So what other things do we attract in our life? Well we attract lessons. Lessons such as when we are driving and we look around and see all these really bad drivers. Could it be you? Someone may be saying the same thing about you as you drive. Let's face it many of us are not always paying attention to the road when we are driving. So what's the lesson here? Maybe it's something as simple as learning to turn off the anger and turn on the patience and let them be who they are. They have their own lessons to learn. Perhaps they are just showing you a side of how you drive that you don't want to see. But these are things that you need to figure out.

Another example of lessons to be learned is this. You're on your third marriage or long-term relationship and you're wondering why you're considering moving on. Can you figure out why? Remember you chose that person; he/she didn't force you into this relationship. So what is the common element here? That's right, it is you. Now this doesn't make you a bad person, it just means that each of these people was, or possibly still is, in your life so you get to work through those issues that hold you back from realizing your full potential and how to be really great, so you're next relationship is beautiful. But you have to understand that it's not just their fault.

There are many places where we may encounter an uncomfortable situation. So what do you do with this circumstance? Do you look at it as an outsider, without emotion, and consider how to deal with it? Do you get emotionally charged and fight for your beliefs, just to be right; or do you listen to your inner voice, not the ego, and see from a new perspective? What are you paying attention to, where is your focus and what is the outcome you desire? Is it to be right or to be at peace?

Here's where you have an opportunity to be great. Now is the time to pay attention to your higher self; rise above the reaction and the lashing out or the need to be right. Listen to your inner being, and take action by being compassionate and coming from a place of love and peace. Pay attention to those things and you will receive the gift that you are giving.

Purpose

Wouldn't it be great if life came with a set of instructions? At birth you are handed a book of instructions, which contained al the wisdom of the ages. In some ways this would be great, however you would miss out on some very unique experiences and you probably wouldn't feel like you created anything. From birth you are endowed with all the knowledge to be anything and everything you want to be and have everything and anything you want. Unfortunately, you just don't remember and neither do I. While at birth you can't speak, and you can't really see yet you are communicating to the world what you need and in most cases you receive what you want and need.

Now, I'm sure the question arises in many of you: what about those children who don't get what they need, those who are abandoned, those who are mistreated, those who die prematurely? Why did this happen? Here's where the great debate begins because we are getting into another realm of discussion, perception and belief. Suppose the road we are traveling in this life actually began several lifetimes ago?

I'll give you another perspective from the messages I have received as to why this is. Here's a passage from Michael Berg's book "Becoming Like God." "A rock is hewn from a mountain. It has the same properties as the mountain, but when it is disconnected from the mountain it is no longer called mountain, it is called a rock. Not one atom of its essence has changed, yet pulling it from the mountain has made it something else. Put the rock back into the mountain and it's no longer a rock. So the rock's existence is determined not by it's substance, but by it's relation to the mountain, which is its source.

"Just as rocks are hewn from the mountain so are humans hewn from God. At the level of the soul humans have exactly the same essence as God. In essence humans are like God."

While we all may be like God, each of us has our own purpose for being here and it was you who decided before you came into this life what you would be and why you were coming here. You chose your parents, the time, date and the place. You had and have a purpose and that purpose is to learn how to be one with God and to bring light into the world. Bringing light into the world is different and yet the same for all of us. You bring light into the world by doing something you love and by helping others.

Each of us has a purpose and whatever that purpose is, it is for you discover. Yes, it is everyone. Just as we spoke of earlier with the example of the butterfly flapping it's wings in Japan changing the weather patterns in New York, so every life entering this dimension changes so many lives in so may different ways. Is it hard to comprehend why we have so many people in this world who don't have the luxuries that others have? Is it difficult to understand why there are so many people who are under the rule of the few that have so much power? Of course it is. Yet in all of this seeming lack of equality there are lessons for everyone.

For whatever reason many of us hold that the life a child who is mistreated, unfed and unclothed and left without care is more repulsive than an adult treated or mistreated in the same manner. Why is that? Why do we seemingly value one life more than other? Where do these judgments come from?

I found the following written on a piece of yellow paper between pages 414 and 415 of "A Course in Miracles" as I was searching for thoughts about this. So nothing is an accident or coincidental, it was delivered to me just as I needed it because I intended for it to serve you and me.

"In peace I was created and in peace I do remain. It is given to me to change myself. How merciful is God my father, that when he created me he gave me peace forever? Now I ask to be what I am. And can this be denied me, when it is forever true?"

You and I came here for a reason and it is for you to remember and discover what that is. Perhaps that child that was born into a life of woe and despair is here for others to remember what it is like to feel compassion and use their powers and resources to find a cure for a disease, or to help feed many hungry and underprivileged children. Perhaps in a previous life you were that poor child and now you are born into a family of privilege and you will use your resources to help those in need. I can paint hundreds of scenarios for you, however you must see that everything has a purpose and a reason for being. And as uncomfortable as it may be at this time for you to comprehend you are here to remember, discover, enjoy, assist and be the spiritual being you are while having this human experience. So discover your passion, believe in yourself, pay attention to everything around you and give to yourself and others, love.

Your Body, the Earth – What's common?

Do you take care of your body? Most of us would surely answer yes. At least we like to think we do. Do you eat properly? Do you cook your own meals? Do you eat organic foods? Do you look carefully at the ingredients in processed foods? So just how thoughtful are you of your body, or the instrument you inhabit that allows you to do, be and have?

I'm sure your answers are interesting as well as your reasons for not treating yourself, as you should. I'm not here to chastise you or berate you for not taking care of yourself, because frankly if you don't care about yourself, why should anyone else? That sounds harsh, doesn't it?

By the way, I'm not that kind of person, I'm just creating an awakening here. I'm writing about this for two reasons. One is because I do care about you, and two is because I care about the earth. So what do you and the Earth have in common? Well, you are not just the custodian of your own body; you are the custodian of the earth as well. And frankly I'm concerned that if you don't care about yourself, you won't care about the earth and its other inhabitants, which are your neighbors, your friends, family and me.

Although I can only give you advice on how to take care of yourself, I can't do it for you. But when it comes to the earth we need to work together and we need to understand and come to an agreement. We need to agree that since I want to live a healthy life, you need to be in alignment with me to make it happen. Why? Because I can't do it without you and it's not fair that I have to fight for my life and carry 100% of the burden.

Right now if the earth were your body you would be able to feel how ill it is and how it is suffering. It is suffering with political and economic oppression, war, famine and pollution. Each day there are children all over the world who are suffering from malnutrition, blindness, and homelessness in the hands of heartless people. There are adults who have no idea how to fend for themselves, where to turn for food or shelter and who are slaughtered by tyrants and governments because of greed, political power and religious beliefs.

This is just a call to awakening and as a reminder (although I'm sure you haven't forgotten) that everyday, regardless of what you do, you need not just be aware of how you are a part of, and a caretaker of yourself but also everyone else. I am your brother, your sister, your father, your mother, your aunt, your uncle, and your neighbor on this orb floating in space. Yes, I am your family and we are all traveling in the same bus. We share the same resources and every time you litter, you poison or misuse anything on this earth, whether it be a person, animal or resource you do the same to yourself.

I am on your side, I am looking out for you, I love and care about you and for you; please do the same for me. The atoms that make me who I am and the atoms that make you who you are, are the same, just resonating at different frequencies and they touch each other through the atoms of space and time.

We are so connected - please practice mindfulness and compassion in each moment of your daily life and cultivate peace. With clarity, determination and patience we can all have a peaceful, healthy and prosperous life.

Remembering

This was sent to me today from the Daily Om and it came at just the right time in my writing so I had to pass it on to you.

Most of us are familiar with the idea that we are not human beings having spiritual experiences; instead, we are spiritual beings having human experiences. We hear this and even though we may experience a resounding yes in our bodies, we may not take the time to really acknowledge the truth of these statements. Integrating this idea into how we view ourselves can broaden our sense of who we are and help us appreciate ourselves as brave spirits on an important mission to learn and grow here on earth.

As spiritual beings, we are visitors in this physical realm. The fact that we came here and lost all memory of what happened to us before we were born is one of the many reasons that it takes so much courage for a soul to incarnate on earth. This is why spiritual inquiry so often feels like a remembering, because it is. Remembering that we are spiritual beings is part of the work that we are here on earth to do. When we operate from a place of remembering, we tap into the wisdom that our spirit accumulated even before we stepped into this lifetime.

Remembering who we are can give us the patience to persevere when we become overwhelmed or frustrated. It can give us the courage to work through the most daunting challenges and help us trust the ancient wisdom we carry that is offered to us by our intuition. We have chosen to be on earth because there is something we want to learn that can only happen by inhabiting a body. Some of us are here to repay a debt, learn about love, or teach forgiveness. Most of us are here for a combination of reasons, we carry this information in our souls, and all we have to do is remember. As you go through your journey, try not to forget how brave you are, being here now. Honor yourself.

Throughout this book I will provide reminders that we are connected and that we are spiritual beings because it is in these remembrances that we gain the ability to keep our focus on living in the moment, of being who we truly are, living the rest of our life doing what we are passionate about. That we are all connected, always, and must consider this in our encounter with one another.

Creating Your Reality

Before we end this section on the Law of Attraction I want to cover some questions that typically arise. As you are aware, what you focus on and pay attention to is what will manifest itself in your life. Remember you are the creator of your reality and if that means that you believe that someone will do something to you or for you, you will receive that because it is within your reality. If you give up control of your reality by believing, which is intending, that something is random or uncertain then you have given power to having it be random and unpredictable.

I know this is a difficult concept to grasp but look at your life and the things you have that you wanted and the things that you have that you think you didn't want. Again, these are all within your reality, intended or not intended that's what you receive. YOU MUST BE 100% CERTAIN and you will receive that of which you are 100% certain. No one does anything to you unless you let him or her. Everything I have in my life that I like or dislike I take 100% responsibility for, as I am the one who manifested my destiny and so are you.

You can create, intend and attract what you want into your life, but you must also take action. Sitting on the curb meditating about what you want to attract only works if you later take action. If not, the only action you will see is the moving company coming to your house to take away your furniture.

Tassinello

S.M.A.R.T. is another tool for you to use to achieve your goals.

Specific – Measurable- Achievable- Realistic - Time limited

Specific - Your goal must be clearly defined. Have a specific date to accomplish it by and know what action you will need to take. An example would be the desire to be healthier. Is "healthier"specific? Not really. A specific goal would be to join a health club and/or lose 12 lbs. When you are specific, your goal has a much better chance of being accomplished.

Measurable – Ask the question *"How will I know when it is accomplished?"* The numbers of times you actually go to the Health club or how many pounds you actually loose are measurable goals. Measuring your progress helps you to stay on track to reach your goal. "Wow, I lost 3 lbs this week, I'm right on target!"

Attainable – It is wonderful to set high goals, but be realistic about them. Setting goals that are unrealistic can be very disempowering. Good example: "I have lost 12 lbs in 3 months." Bad Example: "I will lose 12 lbs by *next week.*" Again you must see it as done.

Realistic – This is being realistic with a stretch. You may have a good grasp on what it will take to reach your goals, however are the resources you need available and affordable? Can you get them in the time frame necessary? Is what you are about to create timely and wanted or needed? However you answer these questions be sure that you add some stretch. Stretch means either going the extra length to accomplish your goal, or shorten the timeframe to have it accomplished or have backup for the resources you need.

Time limited – Without a time frame, your goal enters that "Nether Land," of someday, or worse that "Never Land," of who knows when. Since you don't want to be Peter Pan in "Never Land" setting a specific end date prompts your unconscious mind to "get to work," now.

Tassinello

Chapter Eleven
The Law of Allowing

My intention is that you understand and use these messages not just for yourself but you use them for the betterment of the world. As with the Law of Attraction each of us creates our own reality, you cannot create someone else's reality. However on a global scale you can allow for others to have a positive experience with you, which creates an opportunity for global wellness. This will happen because you will manifest a positive experience with the people you meet.

The Law of Allowing may be one of the more difficult Laws to get our heads into. First, there needs to be room in your thinking that you already have what you want. I spoke of this earlier. You need to know that there is enough energy in the universe for everyone's complete happiness. As I say this remember that you cannot create another person's reality, however you can show up as how you want your reality with them to be as a co-creator.

There is an enormous amount of freedom in allowing people and circumstances to be who or what they are, whether you agree with them or not. And it doesn't matter what we are talking about or what is going on in the world. Are you kidding me here? You mean I'm supposed to allow war, disease, crime or poverty? Well, yes and no. First you can't change someone else's reality, although creating a positive interaction with them may change their perception, thus changing their reality. The fact is this, if you wage war on crime or wage war on disease or wage against war you are just giving it power and attention. Even if you are focused on being against it you are as well attracting it because it is in your consciousness. You are manifesting the thought of war, whether you are for or against it matters not. If you take war out of the news, out of your consciousness it is more likely you will never see war.

Here's one of the places we get stuck and here's where ego plays the mind game. If you are creating reality at every moment then is what you are creating really what you allowing or what the ego makes you believe you are allowing? Jealousy and envy are powerful tools of the ego. Watch closely as to what you think you are allowing without controlling.

Now remember we are talking about you, not them, and not what is happening around you. Your attention and focus must be positive and one of allowing others to be themselves and make their own discoveries.

Removing Doubt, Allowing Change

As an example, I found it difficult to allow partners in a relationship to be themselves. I thought I did but the truth is that I wanted to be in control. How I thought, what I intended and the attention I paid to it was not that I would change, but that my partner would. I didn't remove the doubt I had about allowing her to change. Yet, after our breakup it became clearer to me what my part in our relationship was as a co-creator. I know that it seems strange that I could work on having a better relationship after the fact, but that's part of life and part of seeing, changing and growing. Be grateful for recognizing your lesson whenever it comes to you as I am now. At least you made it to a place of understanding so your next relationship will be better and grow.

Now my focus was on my being kind, not on her action or how I saw her action or, more importantly how I thought she would show up. I focused my intention on allowing us an opening, an opening to change and to having a pleasant giving relationship and one that allowed me to see her as loving and pleasant. It took a while, but I was the one who needed to change my perception, my intention and myself.

I could view the years we spent together as wasted or I could view them as being in school to learn from her (she being my teacher) and I chose the latter. There is great peace in knowing that I have identified some of the lessons I needed to learn to have peace, tranquility and love. She is a fine woman and we have a better relationship now, although we have each chosen to be apart, we have also chosen love and peace and allowing. As well we have both chosen to move on to new chapters in our lives.

It's like this, if all of us turned our attention to positive thoughts with the intention that every encounter would be fun and loving and caring then that's the way it would be. In other words the more consciously selective you are about where you choose to focus your attention, instead of going into resistance, the more positive your encounters will be.

Artificial Appearances

The appearance of something is a wonderful magician, an extraordinary deceiver, capable of convincing our hearts and minds of the strangest lies. How often do we choose our clothes, houses, jobs, friends and mates by the most superficial standards?

How many times have you chosen a partner strictly by appearances, or purchased a new car or home only to keep up appearances? Really consider your choices by wanting a healthy relationship or a healthy body or for your work to be fulfilling. Be deliberate and intend it, feel it, focus on it and pay attention to it. Your emotions will always let you know if you are in a place of allowing, so pay attention to them, they are your guides.

I know how difficult this can be because there is this part of us that wants to fix things that we believe are wrong or unjust. We want to fix poverty, we want change criminals, we want to eliminate war, we want to change so many things based on our beliefs and perceptions. Unfortunately all we can do is give attention to making positive impacts by providing a space for allowing and withholding judgment. I am not suggesting we condone any negative action, but we must not judge, lest we be judged.

All we can do is show up as tolerant, non-judgmental, and support others rights in allowing them to be who they are. As difficult as this may seem, if everyone did this can you then see peace, love and tranquility? Do not say yes, I can see that with a "but;" because it is the "but," that puts you in the middle of confrontation. It is the "but" that negates everything you just said or agreed to.

When you have an emotional reaction to someone else's behavior, stop and tell yourself; he/she is neither good nor bad. I neither like him nor dislike him. She is just another human being doing the best she can. Given his conditioning, his beliefs, his circumstances, his present needs and desires I might be doing pretty much the same.

Free Will

"Free Will" means everyone has the freedom to do as they please, whether you agree with them or not as long as they don't infringe upon another's freedoms. Just as you believe you have the right to do as you please you must allow others that right as well. To set aside judgment and allow others to be or do, as they will, without trying to fix them, or make them wrong can be challenging.

When you look around at nature do you have judgments about a tree or a plant and to where it is growing or what it does? "I really don't like where that mountain or lake is located so let's move it." As most of us would agree nature is perfect and needs no help from humans. If you are okay with nature why then can you not hold the same attitude toward other people? Your getting angry or upset will do nothing to change another and those negative feelings you are harboring effects only you.

Each of us is whoever we are and we must see we cannot change someone else's nature. Short of violence, force, lies or deception we cannot change anyone. Even if you try they will still remain who they are. As Ben Franklin said, "A man convinced against his will is of the same opinion still." Is manipulation the way you would have someone change? When you accept peace, then you will find peace and by making it manifest you will see peace.

If you try to beat a thought into someone and try against his or her will to change his or her perception, you cannot. The point is that if we attempt to apply the standards of sensual perception in an attempt to understand our position and role in the Universe, we will necessarily fall far short of learning anything of much importance. Inner growth comes to us through our inner universe not from our perceptions of the material world around us reported by our senses.

While you may not agree, here is an example. President Obama extended an invitation to Iran to sit down and discuss how we might work together. The was a first step towards peace and if Iran truly wants peace they can manifest it. You cannot make peace by making war. You can't bring peace through warlike actions. You bring peace through peaceful actions. And you cannot ask for peace while preparing for war. The US created an opening for peace and if peace is truly the intention and we pay attention to making peace it will become manifest.

Opportunity

The law of allowing enables us to powerfully and passionately permit our focus to become a reality. We were born into an environment where we all have choices. This is the beauty of our world, which gives each of us the opportunity to find our passion. You are here to work on yourself. If there are things you would prefer were different then you should be thrilled to know that you can create that reality as well. It is a process of continual growth. By changing the way you act with others it changes the way they act with you.

It saddens me when I think how often we seek happiness from things outside of ourselves, when happiness resides within us. As I say this, I smile as I feel all the happiness I was endowed with when I entered this world. We are all born with the same spiritual resources. It is so important to not seek the approval of others for our self worth. I want you to think about how often you need, or look, for people or material things to make you happy.

Wow, I just can't wait to buy something new, all the joy it will bring me. Is that joy and happiness for a moment, for a day, a week, or a month? Or how about when you meet someone new and you feel that special connection and all of a sudden you want to be with them a lot. Then you think of how happy you will be with them, how they will complete your life. In reality they won't complete your life and they can't give you happiness, but they could add to your joy, excitement and happiness.

The things that will bring us happiness are within us. Liking and loving ourselves because of who we are and the good things we do by giving love through helping, teaching, or providing assistance to others, with compassion and care. True happiness resides in what you do for others. As you give, so shall you receive.

Every day take time to be still and reflect on the day and understand any lessons you may have gained from the day's experiences. Quiet your mind and relax your body. Meditate and clear your mind and let the thoughts flow freely as if you were on a train and you were watching the scenery go by and do not give attention to any one thought or scene.

"No thought, no action, no movement, total stillness: only thus can one manifest the true nature and law of things from within and unconsciously, and at last become one with heaven and earth."

Lao Tzu

I hope the following point will help you throughout life as you communicate with anyone.

"Watch your thoughts, for they become words.

Watch your words, for they become actions.

Watch your actions, for they become habits.

Watch your habits, for they become character.

Watch your character, for it becomes your destiny."

There is this force in the universe, within you, which is called the "Desire to Receive for the Self," it's called ego (everybody's got one). It is a state that we inhabit virtually all of the time and it is the source of our pain and suffering. Knowing this and recognizing that it exists, is one of the first steps in overcoming this force. The ego has a dualist personality, one that keeps us competitive and one that puts us at odds with others. You need to understand your ego and keep it in check.

Kabbalah teaches that as rocks are hewn from mountains, so are humans hewn from the Light. At the level of the soul humans have the same essence as the Light. So in essence we are a piece of the Light. Let your light shine through love and understanding.

Creating A Crack In The Prison Wall

I know many of us have heard the term "Think outside of the box." It has been used with some success in business to step outside of your usual way of thinking about how you believe things are, how they exist and how things will turn out. This is where you have an opportunity to make that "Quantum Shift." Not just to think outside the box, but to create a crack in your prison wall.

Most of us live in a prison; it's this room with no windows and no doors. It's this place where we have all of our beliefs and perceptions about our self and we have no idea that we can actually make a door and walk out into another realm. We are living in our own prison, so to speak.

There are no guards and no one to keep you inside this room except you and how you think. Now what if I told you there is a way out, that there is a crack in these walls or that there is a hidden door just waiting to be discovered? Are you willing to seek it out? Are you willing to make a great effort to break free from this room, this prison and see all the beauty of the universe and share it with all the other beings outside of your prison?

It takes a real commitment to break free from the pain and suffering you have caused yourself and bask in the light of joy and happiness. You can transform yourself from living in your limited world of the ego and begin living from your soul through giving to others.

If it seems we are getting off track from all the Laws we are talking about I assure you we are not. The Laws are here to be recognized as tools to get you to think differently and to know that you can act differently and achieve the harmony of life we all deserve. But you also must recognize and admit what you have created where you presently reside and that you may not be living within this circle of life and love.

The ego nature wants you to believe that desire for the self is natural, and that if you don't go after these things selfishly you will never attain those things you believe, or the ego wants you to believe, are important and necessary for your happiness. I challenge you to do the following for one week. But you must be committed to doing this without hesitation and without reservation.

For one week, do not think of anything you want. Wake up each morning with a smile, know that you feel good and rested, take deep breaths and relax. Each day for this week do whatever anyone else wants, do not argue, and do not make suggestions for changing what they want whether at home or at work.

If someone asks for your advice provide it with love and think about the other person and act from how you would want to be treated before you reply. In every instance think before you act and DO NOT REACT. Every act during this week will come from love and not from "what's in it for me." Each day I want you to note how this day is different from your usual day and how people are being around you.

Freedom

The Law of Allowing is not just about allowing others to be themselves but also for you to allow you to be yourself. To illustrate this point I use this story about a spiritual leader, from the book "Becoming Like God" written by Michael Berg.

"When I was eleven, he said, I was a lost cause as a student. I never minded my teachers and I played hooky from school at every opportunity. Then one evening, I heard my parents in the next room talking about me. My mother was

crying.

"What are we going to do with our son?" she said to my father. "He has no interest in his studies. He doesn't want go to school, and any day now they will expel him. Then what will become of him?"

"As I listened to her, a strange event occurred: I could feel her anguish as acutely as if it had been my own. I burst into the room and I told her I was sorry. I promised that I would be a good student and obedient from that moment on. I made the promise not because I cared about studying but because I cared about my mother and did not want to cause her pain. I kept my word and changed my ways. I became studious and never missed a day of school, and I grew up to be the scholar you see before you now.

"My point is this: If I had not overheard my parents that day, what would have become of me? Well, I would have been a good person, since it was in my nature to do so. I would have prayed, I would have given to charity; I would have enabled many others to earn a good living.

However, imagine what would have happened after I left this world and arrived in the place called the "heavenly court."

"My judges would say, "Where are your thousands of students?"

"I would gape at them and reply, "What are you talking about? I was a merchant and I did good business, but I didn't have any information to impart to even a handful of students, let alone thousands. Let's talk instead about the sums of money I gave to charity."

"And then they would say, "Where are the dozens of books you were supposed to write?"

"Again, I'd look at them as if they were unhinged. "What do you mean, 'dozens of books? I wasn't illiterate—I could read and write—but I had no reason to write any books; I had nothing to teach anyone. Let's talk instead about the many kindnesses I bestowed on my friends, my family, and my customers."

"Then they would show me everything I could have achieved, everything I should have done. Can you imagine the grief I would feel in that moment? There is no greater hell than to see what we might have done, but in fact failed to do.

So do not measure yourself against someone else, measure yourself against who you want to be. What is your potential? And do not let anything stop you from becoming who you were meant to be. It does not matter at what age or the circumstances under which you seem to be or what anyone else has to say about you and who you could become. Do not let anything stand in the way of your receiving the greatest gift of all, which is for you to realize your potential and to live your destiny.

It's Not About what You Do

In our search to define ourselves, we often look to what we do to show us our worth. Society does not judge all professions equally, however, and it is not uncommon for the individuals who hold what others may consider to be ordinary or menial jobs to feel that they themselves are ordinary or menial. Yet, in truth, many wonderful and wise people throughout history have held what have typically been perceived as ordinary jobs, and this in no way has had any bearing on whether or not they have managed to contribute their skills and talents to the world.

Whether you work in business, education, medicine, retail, or another profession, your worth is inherent to who you are and not what you do for a living. A job that you enjoy, lets you meet your needs, and allows you to live in accordance with your values will always be more gratifying than a high-status job that you dislike. But while experiencing professional satisfaction can be a vital part of being fulfilled, it is important to remember that it is possible to find happiness in any job. Your attitude and intention can turn a mediocre job into work that fulfills you because of the way that you approach it. How you do your job will set you apart from those who care little about how they do the same job as you.

If you do your job well and what you do benefits others, then you are doing work that is making this world a better place. If you are happy in your current line of work and feel that it allows you to be yourself and live authentically while meeting your emotional and physical needs and allowing time for you to enjoy the fruits of your labor, then you have found a job that adds value to your life. If you are a waitress, then be the best waitress you can be, take pride in your work and others will notice your passion. You can contribute your talents and skills to this world while doing any job. It is not the kind of work you do that allows you to be of service. It is you who must choose to be of service through the work that you do.

Fear of Success and Failure

There is a quote from the movie, "What Happens in Vegas", which really underscores how we avoid making changes and getting what we want in life, and it goes like this:

"If you stop betting, you never have to loose"

It just points out that most of us never really take a risk. I'm not saying you should go to Las Vegas and begin gambling or take some other uncalculated risk. Sometimes we're afraid of losing and other times we're afraid of success. Life is meant for living and experiencing, giving and sharing, and learning and teaching.

The next time you tackle a project or say you're going to do something, stretch yourself. If you think you can comfortably run 5 miles a day, then run 6 or 7 miles the next time you go for a run. If you don't stretch yourself you'll never know what your full capabilities are. This is exactly how winning athletes win, by always moving beyond their best, stretching until they're all stretched out. If you don't do this you will never know just how great you can be.

Here's another part of allowing: allowing yourself to be, to question what you have learned through institutions, organizations, the media and the government. As well being open to other people's ideas, beliefs, perceptions, and teachings.

There is so much to learn, see and experience while we are here on this earth. So it is necessary to understand that we don't always have the right answers. Without listening, or reading or searching we block our awareness from learning. If you ever make judgments about someone because you think you are smarter than they are you have closed yourself off from learning more. You may be smarter in some things, but you can't know everything. You never know what you could learn unless you are open to allowing. You may be smart but also try to be wise.

So how do you sort through all the information available and that you are typically bombarded with each day? That's where your spirit guide comes through and leads you to what is correct for you. Your life is meant to be joyous and happy and although there are times when this is hard to believe and you don't always experience it, it is true. You have all the tools available to you at this very moment to be happy; all you have to do is say so. Just love everything and everyone who comes into your Life today then watch your whole experience change.

We need more of us to see that if we visualize a circle of ten, twenty, a hundred, a thousand or millions of people with each of us massaging the shoulders of the person in front of us we are giving comfort to all with no one left out. Too many times we believe that in giving we will not receive and that is exactly the opposite of how the universe works. That's why I want you to visualize life as a circle. If there are corners or ends then yes, someone is left out and if you think you are the one at the end then not only do you believe you will not receive, and you will be hesitant to give.

A Circle of Love - by Arthur James Tassinello

With each encounter try to listen and understand

To see each others side and to lend a helping hand

Start by greeting one another with love and a smile

Knowing that you did your best and went the extra mile

Cause it's not about winning or needing to be right

It's all about compassion and not about our might

It is a way of being that we know we can adopt

To show love to your neighbor, not just a little but a lot

By giving one another the liberty to be free

We form a Circle of Love for you and for me

A Circle of Love that surrounds us all

A Circle of Love so we each can stand tall

Without fear of reprisals or of scorn or of hate

A Circle of Love, which we can all generate

A Circle of Love bringing freedom and peace

A Circle of Love where we all hold the keys

Can you feel how sharing love embraces us so

So firm yet forgiving it will be all that we know

By keeping this Circle of Love together for us

It gives each of us faith, honor and trust

Through this Circle of Love we'll have a beautiful life

Without war or hate or trouble or strife

Love is always the answer and we are the key

Be in the Circle of Love and bring the world - Joy, Hope and Prosperity

Tassinello

Chapter Twelve
The Law of Benevolence

Benevolence is the expression of kindness and altruism. Benevolence means much good for others. As such, it is a form of love. But some theologians, such as Thomas Jay Oord, have argued that love involves both giving and receiving. A loving person must, then, be both benevolent and open to receiving good or gifts from others.

From Merriam-Webster it is defined as "a disposition to do good, an act of kindness." While the words benevolence and charity are often used interchangeably they are not the same. Being benevolent is to give of yourself and your time, while charity is giving material things and money.

Benevolence is not just about giving it is also about forgiving. Forgiving others for what you perceive was done to you and forgiving yourself for things you perceive as having done to others. I say perceive because it is only our perceptions that give life to all that appears to be.

In A Course in Miracles, there is a passage in Lesson 82. *"The light of the world brings peace to every mind through my forgiveness."*

My forgiveness is the means by which the light of the world finds expression through me. My forgiveness is the means by which I become aware of the light of the world in me. My forgiveness is the means by which the world is healed, together with myself. Let me then, forgive the world, that it may be healed along with me.

The Law of Benevolence places us under an obligation to be a device of happiness to others. Irrespective of their physicality, their race, their creed, their color, their religious affiliation, or their geographical location we have an obligation, a duty, to assist others, whatever their needs. From a simple smile or a kind word to lift someone's spirits to providing food, shelter or goods.

Benevolence in a sense is a sub category of charity and no other area of life demonstrates the major kabbalistic teachings more clearly than giving and receiving. True giving or charity is not the thing we do once a year for a tax write-off to earn a deduction. Benevolence should be a fundamental part of daily living. It is definitely necessary for the transformation of the giver with its focus not just on the physical results, but also on the spiritual effects.

Transformation By Giving

The overriding characteristic of giving is the power it has to transform us from the physical world of the desire to receive for the self alone to recognize not just the importance of being charitable, but for the gaining of a connection to the Light.

Anytime we give of ourselves, whether it is time, goods or money we bring ourselves closer to peace and the Light. Although we know we are giving to receive, because it is the only way to receive, we do it not just from the aspect of receiving but because it is in our nature and spirit to do so. Only self-less giving will get you the rewards you so deserve. It can't be contrived.

Receiving gifts are as important as giving as long as we receive this charity with the consciousness that we are bringing Light to the person who gives to us. Through receiving we are providing the giver with an opportunity to perform a noble act.

Here is an analogy from Michael Berg. "When there are no guests at the inn, the innkeeper has nothing to do. He cannot express his desire to be a good host or his talent for doing so. But when a guest finally arrives, the innkeeper is able to fulfill his nature. Far from feeling burdened by the guest, the innkeeper is grateful for the opportunity that has been provided. When the guest departs, the innkeeper can truly say, "Whatever I have done for you, you have done more for me." With an awareness of this paradigm, receiving charity can be understood as a righteous action equal to that of giving it.""

Where we get stuck often, as I have done in the past, is to think or get the impression that money is bad. Money is only a tool; a piece of paper that we have decided has value. It is no more valuable than cattle or sheep or cars as something to trade for something else. We have made money the predominant medium for trade. It becomes a problem when it is idolized above all else does. When it becomes greater than your love of others or of God, then it becomes a bad thing.

If you see it as only a tool to provide for other things in your life then it is used properly. Idolizing anything but the Light or God will provide you only sadness. If you give and receive money, as you would love, smiles, encouragement, kind words or hugs then you are using it, as you should for your highest good. So giving can come in many forms as long as what you do with it and how you give it come from your heart.

Chasing Rabbits?

For many years my life was built around the dollar and one of the reasons why I have had so many issues with relationships, and wealth. I was like a greyhound dog at a racetrack; except I wasn't chasing a rabbit I was chasing the greenback. It really didn't matter much to me what I did to make money, nothing illegal of course, but as long as I knew that I could make more than I was making at my last job or business I would be ready to make a change and run as hard as I could after it.

I got my first job at the age of 14 and during these past 50 years I've worked for 26 companies and have owned or been a partner in 9 other ventures. My titles ranged from clerk, to store manager, electrician, engineer, timekeeper, salesman, branch sales manager, district sales manager, regional sales manager, marketing manager, director for strategic partners, sales director, vice president of sales and marketing, and president and CEO. While money was my motivation

I had some incredible experiences, learned a lot about many businesses and managing people and myself.

These were adventurous and tumultuous times and while managing the paper end of a business was easy; it was the personal and business relationships that took work and where I had to learn more about compassion and commitment.

I realized I lacked certain sensitivities when it came to getting a job done and communicating that to others, as well balancing work with my personal life. Work always won the battle for my attention and too many times I treated my relationships as if they were an employee.

Each time I had a problem or an issue with business I had a tendency to take out my frustration and angst on the person closest to me. Even when I was studying spiritual material I would be better for a while but went right back to old habits. I idolized money to the point where I couldn't see what the light was all about. The other problem was that I thought that in order to be spiritual I had to be poor and if I wanted to be rich I couldn't be spiritual. So my greed and ego usually won that battle.

So many years fighting with myself, which of course is the purpose of the ego. Each time I went broke and was studying spiritualism the message was clear. Arthur this is your chance to have both if you would just get the message. What message? You mean the message to put on a white rob and live in a commune without women and without money? Or the message that said, "forget about being spiritual go for the big bucks." You'll have so much more fun. I was a puppet and my ego the puppet master.

Well, I could say it took long enough, but here I am with a true understanding of my passion and who I am, and who I am meant to be and choose to be. I can look at the past and have regrets or I can look at the past and be grateful for all I have learned. I have managed to get to where I am today with having had so many amazing experiences.

In addition I have asked others for their forgiveness, I have forgiven others who I thought harmed me and I have forgiven myself. Perhaps it has taken me longer than someone else, but I am grateful for finding peace. As they say, "better late than never."

Today, I can smile and laugh at myself and be grateful for everything I have and have learned. Because everything I have that has real value is all the people I have met, loved and cared for and who are still in my life today as a son and daughter, former spouse(s), sister, in-laws, cousins, aunts, uncles, nieces, nephews, friends and colleagues. These are my true and lasting rewards, the rewards of love and friendship. All of these wonderful, beautiful and thoughtful people with whom I have received so many lessons and gifts.

So what I write about is one of my gifts to you. This is giving you the opportunity to see what life was like for me, perhaps similar to yours and all that life has to offer. You can choose now to learn from my experiences and use my knowledge and my wisdom to avoid so much of life's drama and have a more comfortable life starting now. You can have fun, lots of money, great health, and terrific relationships just by relating to my experiences and now begin to test the waters yourself by using the principles in this book to help and guide you. Hopefully this will make your life a little easier.

Let the Waters Flow

The following narrative from The Daily Om is a powerful story that says so much about who we are and how life works. Now, if we can be like the river our lives would be less constraining and strenuous.

The journey of water as it flows upon the earth can be a mirror of our own paths through life. Water begins its residence on earth as it falls from the sky or melts from ice and streams down a mountain into a tributary or stream. In the same way, we come into the world and begin our lives on earth.

Like a river that flows within the confines of its banks, we are born with certain defining characteristics that govern our identity. We are born in a specific time and place, within a specific family, and with certain gifts and challenges. Within these parameters, we move through life, encountering many twists, turns, and obstacles along the way just as a river flows.

Water is a great teacher that shows us how to move through the world with grace, ease, determination, and humility. When a river breaks at a waterfall, it gains energy and moves on, as we encounter our own waterfalls, we may fall hard but we always keep moving on. Water can inspire us to not become rigid with fear or cling to what's familiar. Water is brave and does not waste time clinging to its past, but flows onward without looking back.

At the same time, when there is a hole to be filled, water does not run away from it in fear of the dark; instead, water humbly and bravely fills the empty space. In the same way, we can face the dark moments of our life rather than run away from them.

Eventually, a river will empty into the sea. Water does not hold back from joining with a larger body, nor does it fear a loss of identity or control. It gracefully and humbly tumbles into the vastness by contributing its energy and merging without resistance. Each time we move beyond our individual egos to become part of something bigger, we can try our best to follow the lead of the river.

Looking again at benevolence and its role in your life, this sharing is an opportunity for you to experience a certain consciousness of affluence and fairness, rather than destitution and scarceness. Always remember that it is not the amount that you give, but it is the meaning with which you give.

The Heart of The Matter

There are countless stories of people who have endowed hospitals and charities with millions of dollars. When we hear of this we say, "wow, isn't that so magnificent." Not to downplay such a huge gift to a noble cause, but is that anymore or any less noble than someone, who has barely enough for themselves and shares the little they have with someone else. Perhaps in some respect that is a larger gift or gesture of kindness than the billionaire who gave away millions.

In the end whatever you give is good, and the right amount, as long as it hurts a little bit.

The power of self-sacrifice and true sharing is awakened in the cosmos through thoughtful action. The motivation for sharing doesn't come from moral or ethical values, not that you shouldn't have morals or ethics, but more to the point of being motivated to do so with an attitude of creating good relationships with someone. The more we give with motivation to do so from our heart the more the Light of the Creator bestows upon us.

Giving is a way to receive, but only if it hurts a little or a lot because then you are giving because you really want to, not because you have to or because you will get something in return or because it's easy or expected. What's really interesting about this, now that you know it, is even if you are giving from your heart you will question yourself and constantly wonder if you really did it to get something back. I do assure you that you will know the difference.

What we're trying to accomplish here is to make you aware of what you can do to bring light to yourself and into the world. Is it easy? Hell no, it's hard. That's why you need to work at being introspective. You must look at everything you do everyday with every encounter. Once you really align with the universe and the Light there is no turning back, I promise you. Remember thoughts are as powerful as an outward physical action.

From now on you will look at everything you do; and if there is some doubt about what you just did or are about to do, you will think twice. If it was uncomfortable, if you think you needed to do something differently then for sure you did need to do it differently. Now would be the time to immediately correct your action or act in another way, a way that you know would be correct and coming from your higher self. There are no more excuses when you reach this pinnacle of knowing.

We have talked a lot in this section about giving and mostly from the sense of giving money, material things and of your time. What I believe is as important is giving up of your ego and living from correctness. We all instinctively know right from wrong; it's in our DNA. Even those who are labeled as criminals and have done things that are atrocious know that what they did was wrong. Whatever the reason or the excuses they make to themselves or their justification for wronging another, they know without a doubt it was wrong.

Really Getting It

But what about the little things you do? I mean the tiniest of things you do, which some of you will call a "white lie." Do you really think that's okay? I mean is there some scale of wrongdoing that's acceptable? Is there? I'd like to insert a long pause here so you really have time to cogitate over this.

Now that you've had some thought about that I want to tell you what its like when you really get it and I mean really get it. What I'm talking about is getting to the point where you know every single itty bitty time you are about to do something that's out of character or alignment with the Light. That's right, every time. It smacks you in the head like a baseball bat every single time. This happens because every thing that you do, once you get the picture, is think about every thing you do.

For most of our lives we do stuff that let's say is a little or a lot hurtful to someone else. We tell lies; sometimes we call them white lies, as if there is a difference. There are the lies we tell because we say don't want to hurt someone else. You know the one where Mary asks you this question, "Have you seen our friend Claire recently?" You say "No I haven't seen Claire in days." Which is not true because you saw Claire with Mary's husband from a distance the other day and not knowing whether Claire was aware of this or not, you lie to Mary.

How about when your wife asks you why you're late from work and you tell her you had last minute details to take care of when you actually went to a bar with your colleague for a drink and a chat. There are the lies about what you spent on clothes, where you were, what you were doing and more. How about talking about someone behind his or her back. Stealing any amount of money from a quarter to millions of dollars. Telling someone you care for him or her when you don't because you say I don't want to hurt his or her feelings.

There are all kinds of excuses and reasons for why we are dishonest. However, the lies that really hurt us the most are the ones we tell to ourselves. Where we make believe we are happy or content or we are doing our job, when we are not. That we like what we do when we don't. That we say we are okay with our physique or our health, when we are not.

You cannot and will not be wealthy, in this case have well-being, if you keep up with the lies and cheating and stealing and being dishonest in any way with yourself or someone else. When you really get it you will question everything you do and this is a very good thing. Now you can create the life you have always wanted and you can make intentions and pay attention to them and be benevolent because it is the truth. As Martin Luther King once said, "The truth will set you free."

Giving to Receive

This is being benevolent to yourself as well as others. Benevolence is the performance of a good or charitable act without seeking a profit. Why not perform a charitable act for your soul? Treat yourself with more respect. Experience little or no guilt for the rest of your life. That's what being benevolent to yourself is all about. It's not just about giving to others it's about doing the right things, which provide you with the respect you deserve. If you can really respect yourself, then you have earned the respect of others. I'm not talking about the kind of respect you get, or you think you deserve, because you became monetarily wealthy. Real wealth is about well-being and well-being is about having harmony in all areas of your life.

So why do we spend so much time talking about all of these laws? Why can't you just spell it out for me? Just tell me what to do and I'll do it so I can have all the things I want in life. Wouldn't that be fabulous if all you had to do was to do whatever anyone else told you and your life would be perfect. I know you're really laughing right now because that is so absurd. Isn't it? First, why would you believe what I have to say?

There are plenty of people out there that will tell you what to do everyday of your life. Is that what you want? What you want is to follow the Laws that I speak about, and what the sages and gurus and other teachers have been telling you about for eons. These are the only laws that exist and you have been given free will to follow and use them for your own good and the good of the planet.

Like you I have helped others either physically, mentally or monetarily. When you know that intentionally giving to receive is from the ego it's still a good thing, however it is better to give from your heart not needing to receive as this brings more light into the world.

Real sharing is a little counterintuitive to our nature. It takes work. You just don't read this and then all of a sudden you're benevolent. It's sort of like losing weight. You know what to do and how to do it, however if you don't do what you need to do every day you're not going to lose the weight, are you? Everybody wins when both parties give from compassion and appreciate the receiving. It creates that circle I spoke of earlier where you are always getting as you are giving.

I know I can get very repetitive but it takes repetition for us to learn. In order to get the message, in order to understand and apply the lessons we need to be told at least six times. That is a proven scientific fact. So perhaps I'll tell you the same thing a few more times using different words, analogies or through anecdotes or metaphors. I mean, you do want to know, don't you?

Opening Your Heart

It is not easy to have an open heart in a world that offers us a full plate of experiences just for the taking. This life gives us much joy, love, and light, but it also shows us a fair amount of pain, sadness, and suffering. When our hearts are open, we take everything into ourselves, and we are deeply affected by what we see. We do not hold ourselves separate from the pain of others. In addition, our own personal disappointments may begin to take their toll. We may feel small, alone, and overwhelmed. Most of us may feel like we are not up to the task of living with our hearts open, and we might begin to close down, little by little, so that we can get through our days without having to feel too much pain.

One thing that can help us turn this situation around is an awareness of the power of empathy. To open our hearts to another persons suffering is a revolutionary act that has energetic implications. Many experiments with meditation have proven that we can reach far beyond the boundaries of our selves and heal others when our hearts are open. Heart meditations awaken this power and heal the person meditating, as well as anyone who is the focus of the meditation.

You may want to experiment with this the next time you see or hear something painful. Instead of shuttering your emotions, resolve to hold your feelings in your heart. Tap into the divine energy of universal love that resides in your heart. This energy makes you powerful, for it is your protection that will transmute the pain of others. Breathe deeply, and let yourself feel the pain of the situation, knowing that your heart is big and strong enough to hold it. As you breathe, visualize healing light emanating from your heart and touching all who are suffering. You will heal your heart in the process.

Here are few ways to be benevolent. I suggest you make your own list, as well.

- **Smile** – Smiling allows others to smile and think about having a great day and probably passing it on to others.

- **Be kind** – It takes so little to consider others even if they are not considerate of you. Use words of kindness or encouragement.

- **Give Time** – Give your time, your undivided attention to those you love, especially your immediate family. Spend some quality time with employees, colleagues, and even competitors to show them you want to help and care about your relationship.

- **Be authentic** - Give because you mean it, not because someone told you to.

- **Share** – To connect with the Light and not from a self-serving desire.

- **Give Money** – It's okay to give money, but be sure that it is given not as an easy method to escape from giving of yourself and give enough that it makes you a little uncomfortable.

- **Ego** – Everyone's Got One - Keep your ego in check and that means check it at the door. Competing EGOs always lose.

- **Receive** – Receive charity with the consciousness that you are bringing the Light to the person giving to you. Remember the innkeeper. You are giving them the opportunity to perform a righteous action.

Chapter Thirteen
The Law of Tithing

Similar to benevolence is tithing, with the exception that it's mostly about giving material things, your hard earned money, the stuff that is usually the most difficult to share. There are many definitions of when tithing started, which religions used tithing and when they began asking for tithes. While most religions speak of tithing as necessary and required, it is not a demand, but a recommendation that a person tithe 10% of their income.

So why is tithing important? Is it a tool of abundance and protection? Or, is it a necessary or unnecessary annoyance? Well, a tithe is giving 10% of your income to another and it is built into the fabric of the universe. It is a matter of science and not religion.

When a person tithes, the universe that works under the spiritual law of tithing says, "If you have that much to give, that means you are open to receive more."

As humankind fulfills its part of the covenant by giving 10 percent to God, then God fulfills its part by continually blessing us. So, you may want to check it out with a joyful attitude of saying, "Lord, I am open to receive whatever it is that you bless me with," and then discover for yourself the blessing of fulfilling God's covenant.

Ten Dimensions

If you ask most Quantum theorists and most ancient sages they will both agree that the universe has ten dimensions and ten energy levels. In essence there are ten different versions of you. The one version you know as you is the person who receives emails and letters and is sent bills from your utility company. Then there are the other potentials of who you are possible to be as you attain higher levels of consciousness and prosperity.

The universe is like a department store with ten levels and you can choose which floor you want to be on. The catch is that in order to get to the other floors you have to clean up your 1% existence.

This is a good time to review what we talked about earlier, which is that the universe is 99% energy or light. That means everything from your home to your car to the things in your office and in your garage is energy, as we know, just all vibrating at different energy level. This is called the electromagnetic zero-point field of the quantum vacuum or the "Zero Point" field for short. The "Zero Point" refers to the fact that even though this energy is huge, it is the lowest possible energy state. All other energy is over and above the zero-point state.

Bernard Haisch in his paper "Brilliant Disguise" discusses in more detail Newton's equation and Mach's principle which has to do with the equation $F=ma$. What I love about all of this scientific jargon is that Haisch summarizes it this way; "To put it in somewhat metaphysical terms, there exists a background sea of quantum light filling the universe, and that light generates a force that opposes acceleration when you push on any material object. That is why matter seems to be the solid, stable stuff that our world and we are made of."

So why do I bring this up again? Because, I want to validate the fact that science and spirituality are indeed on the same page. Whether you want to believe in God or the Light or you choose another label doesn't make much of a difference. Whatever words you choose it doesn't cause the feeling. The word dirt doesn't make you dirty any more than the word water makes you wet. The reality is that we, you and I, create everything in our existence.

Greed is Un-Necessary

Human beings are typically greedy, which usually manifests itself in terms of money. We constantly try to amass as much as we can because it appears that there is a limited supply and never enough for us. We always need and want more. You must get out of the "there's only a limited amount of wealth in the universe" mode, "so that's why I can't give away what I have amassed." The resources of the universe are unlimited. There is enough for everyone to be wealthy in all areas of their life and that includes money.

We can break free of this greed pattern by tithing, giving 10 percent of our personal wealth. Tithing activates two levels. One level is here in this world and the other is at the spiritual or invisible level. In the spiritual level you are saying, "You are abundant and handle abundance well, so the universe says, here's some more." When we look at our abundance and contribute joyfully through tithing and are actually cheerful about it, we are expressing a form of splendor of our humanness, and that splendor attracts more abundance.

When we free ourselves of the material realm, it's like giving a "good" infection to others. Instead of greed affecting honest people, honest people start affecting the greedy people. You let go and give, joyfully and unconditionally, bringing light to yourself and the world. It's a way for you to earn your spiritual teachings. If you do it for the joy of giving and lovingly, the abundance starts to come to you in many ways.

After my divorce I began looking at all the STUFF I had accumulated. My ex and I decided that we would trust each other to be fair in dividing up our assets and so I started rummaging through closets, the storage places above the garage and through drawers. I then realized how much we had that was either unnecessary, where we had two or more of the same thing, or things just not used enough to keep. So I began putting things on the side for her or for a garage sale or for charity. It was such a relief to give all these things to someone else who wants them and could use them. It also made me realize how little I actually needed.

There is no need to amass or store things for yourself as the universe has enough for you and will give it to you when you actually need it. Give it and receive it is how the universe works.

Can We Learn to Be Children?

Being generous, feeling unselfish and sharing your possessions, your most treasured items are truly a gift from the heart. When we make a decision to share we open ourselves up to receiving. It puts us in the cycle of abundance and prosperity and it increases receiving in all areas of our life. When we hold back we restrict the flow in our lives because we are acting from fear or need. Be another light in the world, put joy in your heart and in the hearts of others by sharing.

As children we go through stages of differentiation, from thinking that we-are-the-world-and-the-world-is-us to learning that we are separate from each other. Then we learn that there are things that belong to us, and some things that don't belong to us. Soon we learn the idea of sharing these separate things, coming one step back toward the knowledge that we are all part of the same energy. We learn that by sharing, we make other people happy, which makes us happy too. Life brings us many lessons and opportunities on this subject, and we may find it more difficult on some days than others. But today, you can prove that you have learned the lesson well and can even teach others as you enjoy the benefits that sharing brings to your life.

"The service we render others is the rent we pay for our room on earth."

Wilfred Grenfell

When we ourselves are feeling poor it can be a very difficult time to be generous. While some of us have experienced actually being in debt, there are those of us who would feel broke even if we had a million dollars in the bank. Either way, as the old adage goes, it is always in giving that we receive. Meaning that when we are living in a state of lack, the very gesture we may least want to give is the very act that could help us create the abundance that we seek.

Trust in the Flow

One way to practice generosity is to give energy where it is needed. Giving money to a cause or person in need is one way to give energy, but don't give your money conditionally or with the expectation to get it back from the person you gave it to. And don't become angry or resentful if that person doesn't reciprocate. Trust in the natural flow of energy, and you will find yourself practicing generosity with no strings attached, which is the purest form of giving.

Remember that what you send out will always come back you. Selflessly help someone in need without expecting something in return, and know that you too, will receive that support from the universe when you need it. Besides, giving conditionally creates stress because you are waiting with an invisible balance sheet to receive your due. As I said giving unconditionally creates and generates abundance. You must give freely, because you trust that there is always an unlimited supply.

So if you want to know where you stand on tithing, here it is. First, you must acknowledge that money is energy and that Tithing 10% is built into the fabric of the universe. Tithing is the ultimate paradox of the universe, because it means the more you give the more you get. The 10% we give cleanses the remaining 90%. It's like having ten oranges and one goes bad, unless you get rid of the one bad one you risk spoiling the other nine.

So, are you still asking yourself whether to tithe or not? There really is no good alternative. If you keep the 10% the competitor (your EGO) now has access to your life. That money you are holding on to creates a tiny opening for the competitor that he will use to gain entry into your life. If you don't give 10% he can help himself to everything and anything he wants, slowly depleting your assets, whether it is spiritual or monetary. Tithing is a way to buy out your competitor so that he no longer has any say in your business, or your life. So how many of you love having someone else run your life? Just what I thought, no one!

Your New Financial Plan

If you haven't got the picture yet, remember this is a matter of science, not religion. Whether you believe you have enough to give or not, there really is no good alternative. And if you don't give it away (the 10%) to protect the 90% you have, it will be taken from you in some manner. The more you want to get, the more you have to give.

Now you don't have to wait until you give before you start earning the protection of tithing. You can build your tithing into your financial plan. Here's how simple it is.

Let's say you want to earn a million dollars in the next year. Set your plans and tune your consciousness to make $1.1 million. That is building the 10% tithing into your anticipated income. This is a way to properly plan and tune your consciousness to making $1.1 million. You make a plan to share even before you make the money. This is pro-active sharing. You are accessing the light of protection today. You're eliminating the negative forces that are working to take away your money.

Tithing can also protect your well-being, not just your money. Just as there are black holes in space there are black holes in your life. There are people out there that are jealous and envious of you and make disparaging remarks about you. Although conventional wisdom tells us that words can't harm us they do. These words can be so devastating at times; they can be enough to cause us pain and sickness.

Sharing is a good thing, and as you may feel good and people will see you as good, the practicality of tithing is to gain protection from chaos and a lot cheaper that turning your business over to the EGO, who wants to see you suffer. Remember, the EGO wants you to be in turmoil and chaos all the time because if you are, the EGO remains alive and in control. Don't let him take over your life and your finances. Tithe for protection and for your conscience, as the more you share, the more you get, it's the Law.

10 Levels of Giving

- **Level 1 – The Begrudging Giver**

    I don't want to really give, but when I do, I give it grudgingly.

- **Level 2 – The Under Giver**

    I give a lot less than I can afford and a lot less than I should, but I'm happy to make at least some contribution.

- **Level 3 – Reactive Sharing**

    Someone asks me for a favor or someone close to me needs help and I give it.

- **Level 4 – Proactive Sharing**

    I don't need to be asked. I can see when somebody needs help, and I take the initiative to offer him or her, my help.

- **Level 5 – Uncomfortable Sharing**

    This is sharing outside of the comfort zone. This is the correct place to come from. You may never have given to this person before, or it may be more than you feel comfortable with giving, but you do it anyway.

- **Level 6 – Sharing without Recognition**

    This is anonymous sharing. You know where the money is going, but the person or the organization receiving it doesn't know who is giving the gift. This is non-ego sharing and it is ranked very high.

- **Level 7 – Sharing without an Agenda**

    You don't know where the money is going and the receiver doesn't know who it came from. Your giving is arranged through a third party. This is truly high-level sharing.

- **Level 8 – Proactive Action Sharing**

    Here, you cut off someone's pain and suffering before it even happens. You anticipate that a negative situation is about to happen to them, and you share with them so as to avoid the situation rather than waiting until they are in trouble before you help. This is a tremendous level of sharing.

- **Level 9 – Global Scale Sharing**

    You give to a place or an organization that not only takes care of things on a small scale, but also attempts to change the world. This is world-class tithing that can effect changes on a global scale.

- **Level 10 – All of the Above**

    These are the various levels of sharing. Always ask yourself where you stand on the scale, because clarity and truth are the competitor's bitter enemies.

Chapter Fourteen
Harmony and Happiness

The term harmony derives from the Greek ἁρμονία (harmonía), meaning "joint, agreement, concord" and that from the verb ἁρμόζω (harmozo), "to fit together, to join." In Ancient Greek music, the term was used to define the combination of contrasted elements: a higher and lower note.

The definition of Harmony usually pertains to music. However, Harmony in the context of what I am to speak about has to do with Harmony in our lives.

World Harmony

I'll begin with this story about Du Qinglin, vice chairman of the National Committee of the Chinese People's Political Consultative Conference (CPPCC). He spoke at the opening ceremony of the forum in the gigantic Buddhist Palace at Lingshan Mountain and here's what he said. "We anticipate that world Buddhist circles will carry forward the spirit of 'harmony and synergy', manifest the qualities of mercy and compassion, reclaim people's souls and promote harmonious coexistence between humans and nature, humans and society, among people and within each individual.

Du, who is also head of the United Front Work Department of the Communist Party of China (CPC) Central Committee, also said "the world faces financial crisis, social contradictions, culture shock and environmental contamination. To persist in "harmony and synergy" and co-create harmony, we are called upon to depend on the people's welfare, hold high the banner of human progress and create promising conditions for world peace. We should respect diversity on the basis of equal treatment, strengthen mutual understanding

127

through communications and achieve common progress while making up for each other's deficiencies."

Now some of you might ask if I am promoting communism because I printed the quotes of Du Qinglin. I am not promoting anything more in these pages than harmony, and I felt that regardless of Du's stance, politics, affiliation, perceptions and opinions that he expressed a logical and respectful view of Harmony.

Harmony is not just about improving the quality of your life, but also means improving relations with others, regardless of race, creed, color, religion, ethnicity, beliefs, perceptions, opinions, culture, age, or physical attributes.

Can You Make Yourself Happy?

Harmony, whether seeking it for yourself or with others, is really about happiness, and happiness is derived from many things. The very purpose of our lives is to be happy. It is how God wants us to be and it is only us who make life unhappy and disharmonious. It doesn't matter what your religion or even if you are religious, we all want something more and better for our lives.

But why is being happy seemingly so elusive? It is relatively easy to achieve. No don't look so askance at that proposition. You can train yourself to be happy all the time. It is a matter of mind over matter. When you awake in the morning what is your first thought? Is it about what you need to do for the day? Is it about the fact that your alarm didn't go off and you woke up late? Is it that you didn't get good nights sleep? Or, the kids are late and now you have to rush to get them going? Or, or, or any number of other things that you allow yourself to be undone by before you even get out of bed.

This is not about things happening to you. Things don't happen to you, you create them. Regardless of the circumstances of your awakening, you can rise with a smile and a pleasant, if not downright, happy feeling. Look! You are alive! You can make the day start off right without thinking of anything else. Okay so you woke up later than planned. So what! Do you really have to be in a bad mood or are there ways to still manage to get where you need to be on time? And if you are late, then what?

You can bring a certain discipline to your inner being, which means your mind and your spirit. You can transform your attitude, your outlook and your approach to how you live.

Equally Created

Even written in the Declaration of Independence it says, "To which the Laws of Nature and of Nature's God entitle them." Meaning we all have the same entitlements. As well it is written, "We hold these truths to be self-evident, that all men are created equal, that they are endowed by their Creator with certain unalienable Rights, that among these are Life, Liberty and the pursuit of Happiness." Throughout mans history, no matter where you turn or what was written, the basic human need and right is to achieve happiness, not just for oneself but also for everyone.

Why do we attach so much happiness on being wealthy? Is it money that will make you happy? Perhaps money can make you a little happier than you are now, and perhaps not. You can say, "Well, if I had more money I wouldn't have to work as hard or work two jobs, or my wife or husband wouldn't have to go to work, etc., etc." That may well be true and you can do something about that but don't think for a moment that it alone will bring you happiness. Money can bring you some relief and security, but not necessarily happiness.

How about the people who have won the lottery or those who bought shares of stock of a new emerging company for pennies and realized a windfall as the stock rose more than they expected and sold for hundreds of dollars. So how many of them are really happier in their lives now? For a lot of people, winning the lottery is the American dream. But for many lottery winners, the reality is more like a nightmare.

Here are a few stories. "Winning the lottery isn't always what it's cracked up to be," says Evelyn Adams, who won the New Jersey lottery not just once, but twice (1985, 1986), to the tune of $5.4 million. Today the money is all gone and Adams lives in a trailer. "I won the American dream but I lost it, too. It was a very hard fall. It's called rock bottom," says Adams.

"Everybody wanted my money. Everybody had their hand out. I never learned one simple word in the English language – "No." I wish I had the chance to do it all over again. I'd be much smarter about it now," says Adams, who also lost money at the slot machines in Atlantic City.

"I was a big-time gambler," admits Adams. "I didn't drop a million dollars, but it was a lot of money. I made mistakes, some I regret, and some I don't. I'm human. I can't go back now so I just go forward, one step at a time."

Then there is William 'Bud' Post who won $16.2 million in the Pennsylvania lottery in 1988 but now lives on his Social Security. Bud says, "I wish it never happened. It was totally a nightmare."

A former girlfriend successfully sued him for a share of his winnings. It wasn't his only lawsuit. A brother was arrested for hiring a hit man to kill him, hoping to inherit a share of the winnings. Other siblings pestered him until he agreed to invest in a car business and a restaurant in Sarasota, Fla., -- two ventures that brought no money back and further strained his relationship with his siblings.

Post even spent time in jail for firing a gun over the head of a bill collector. Within a year, he was $1 million in debt. He admitted he was both careless and foolish, trying to please his family. He eventually declared bankruptcy. Now he lives quietly on $450 a month and food stamps.

Genetics

So will money bring you a less stressful life or more happiness? Of course it's not the same for everyone but don't look just for money to buy you the happiness you seek. Some researchers have recently argued that an individual's characteristic level of happiness or well-being is genetically determined, at least to some degree.

But even if genetics plays a role in someone's life, how large of a role does it really play? No matter what the scientific evidence says about our level of endowed happiness there are things you can do to enhance your feelings of happiness. Certainly one of the things you can do is to shift your perspective and thinking about how things could be worse.

Blessings In Disguise

It's almost two years since my contracting business began its decline, and about a year since I closed the doors. Within these same two years I finalized my divorce; and my daughter got her license to drive. I had no income, no job, no prospects of getting a job and my house was worth less than I owed. I went in and out of depression and was in a state of constant worry.

Yet as I sit here and write this I am happier than I have ever been before because of my studies and my ability to have faith, trust and belief in the powers of the universe. All of these dilemmas were part of my lessons to find my purpose and passion. It's what brought me to this place of understanding through many people, books, events and occurrences. If it were not for all of these events I would not have found me and would not be able to write with certainty what you are reading.

A friend called me to see how I was doing and as we were talking he said, "Arthur, I don't know how you can be happy now." I explained it to him this way. I said, "Eddie, if it were not for all the problems I have had in the last two years I would not have discovered or read all the books I have and I would not have discovered my true passion in life. I can write this book because I have found answers to happiness and harmony within myself. I am truly grateful for what I have today, which is my health, my intelligence, and my relationships and for all the people with whom I share love and companionship. I still have food on my table, I can still give something to those less fortunate, I can still share what I have with friends and family, and I know that I will be monetarily wealthy again."

Just when someone thinks they really know you, you throw them a curve ball. Of course I want to have more money because it will bring me more creature comforts, but the truth is I don't need to be wealthy. Wealth is the icing on the cake and not the cake. The cake is this entire book. It is the knowledge and understanding I have gained about living a complete and beautiful life, with or without money for there are so many rewards to be had through compassion and love.

I am truly blessed and happy and that doesn't mean I found a new religion, it means I found the connection to the universe, to the Light, to God. God and the Light are here for everyone. We are all connected and I think that you can relate to the evidence all around us. There is no need to be afraid, to doubt, to be depressed or be anxious. Everything you need is here now in this moment, all you need to do is have it.

Now you may say well it is easy for someone who has found it but what about those who haven't and are struggling to find it? Okay, I understand. So maybe it stills feels elusive to you so let's take a look at happiness from the Dalai Lama's perspective.

Another Perspective

The Dalai Lama explains, "Although it is possible to achieve happiness, happiness is not a simple thing. There are many levels. In Buddhism, for instance, there is reference to the four factors of fulfillment or happiness: wealth, worldly satisfaction, spirituality, and enlightenment. Together they embrace the totality of an individual's quest for happiness."

"Let us leave aside for a moment ultimate religious or spiritual aspirations like perfection and enlightenment and deal with joy and happiness as we understand them in an everyday or worldly sense. Within this context, there are certain key elements that we conventionally acknowledge as contributing to joy and happiness. For example good health is considered to be one of the key factors for a happy life. Another factor that we regard as a source of happiness is our material facilities, or the wealth that we accumulate. An additional key element is to have friendship or companions. We all recognize that in order to enjoy a fulfilled life, we need a circle of friends with whom we can relate emotionally and trust."

Now, all of these factors are, in fact sources of happiness. But in order for an individual to be able to fully utilize them towards the goal of enjoying a happy and fulfilled life your state of mind is key. It's crucial.

So where is your mind? Do you recognize all the wealth you already have in your life? Look at, and list, those things about you, and that which you have, that bring you joy. While there is no guarantee that wealth, friends or health will always be in your life to give you the joy and fulfillment you are seeking you can train yourself to experience happiness even when those people or things don't show up on regular basis.

Balance or Harmony?

So what is Harmony really? Harmony is having all parts of your life working to some degree on a positive note. Harmony is when you are paying attention to all areas of your life, not necessarily equally, but when all of them get some attention.

The areas we are speaking about are your finances, health, relationships, mentality and spirituality. In all of these areas we want harmony so that not one of them is neglected. That means you make time each week to work, play, be with your family, improve your mind and your body. This is not the same as balance. When things are in balance that means if you work 8 hours, then you have to play 8 hours and then spend 8 hours with your family and then 8 hours at the gym and then 8 hours reading. In this scenario you would need a 48-hour day, which includes 8 hours for sleep.

On the contrary, harmony means paying attention to each area so none of them are lacking; either your having time with you or with them. It could be going to work for 8 to 10 hours, then to the gym every other day for an hour, spending time with your significant other and/or children a couple of hours a day, or one day a week with them. How about reading and/or meditating an hour a day, or helping others a few hours a week? Whatever time you do spend just be sure of two things. First, make it quality time, not just to do it so you can say, "well, I did it," and second be sure that the other person or you yourself agree that it is significant and time well spent.

Can You Be Content?

We often talk about contentment but what is it that makes us content? Of course, it's different for each of us. However, there is what I will call a "baseline of contentment," which not only satisfies us, it will also allow us to equalize the playing field for the world. Okay, so what does that really mean?

Let's take a deep breath together on this one. Ready? Take a deep breathe in through your nose and then exhale through your mouth. Hold on a second. I just realized that some of you might not know how to take a proper deep breath. No, I'm not kidding. The correct way is to breath in deeply down into your diaphragm, into your belly. So, you're not just expanding your chest, you're breathing in and filling your belly, so you look like you're pregnant. So try one on your own and when you feel it we'll continue on with the exercise and the "equalizing the playing field."

Ready? Great. Let's take 3 deep breathes. Slowly, you are not in a rush. Breathe in through your nose and exhale through your mouth. That's one. Okay now for number two. And now number three. Don't do too many too fast, I don't want you to pass out. This is where you begin to connect with your inner self to achieve inner contentment. Okay, here's what I want you to think about. Do you want to obtain everything that you want and desire; all the money, houses, cars and the perfect mate and body? Or would you rather want and appreciate what you already have? Is this a difficult decision?

Yes, I'm sure some of you are saying "are you kidding me, of course I want the house, car, money, mate and body! That's why I'm reading this." That's unfortunate. Until you begin to appreciate what you have right now, be thankful and in gratitude for what you have at this moment; everything you acquire will never be enough. Your life will never be fulfilled and you will never find true happiness. So, if that's what you want put the book down and find a good novel to read or go watch a movie.

Sometimes It Takes A Tragedy

Unfortunately, for many there must be a personal tragedy in your life before you get the message. Before you understand that there is a spiritual side to life and that all the material things you have amassed only gives you a fleeting moments pleasure. I'm not being sarcastic or cynical. And, it doesn't mean that some of you aren't appreciative of what you have and are spiritual, however you will find that too many people don't live in gratitude, that's why the world is in such chaos.

As you know Christopher Reeve, the actor, had a riding accident and was incapacitated from it and eventually died. In an interview speaking about how he dealt with the trauma and the despair Reeve had this to say, "I had a brief period of complete despair while in the intensive care unit of the hospital." He added "however, those feelings of despair passed relatively quickly, and now he considered himself to be a "lucky guy." He talked about his loving wife and children and also about the rapid advances of modern medicine and how grateful he is because if this accident had happened a few years earlier, he probably would have died from the incident.

He described times when he was troubled by intermittent pangs of jealousy when someone would make a silly passing remark like, "I'm just going to run upstairs to get something." He realized that the only way to get through these feelings was to look at his assets, whatever they are, to see what he can still do and be fortunate about them. Reeve focused on what he had and not what he lacked and became grateful for his ability to use his brain and become a spokesman for and an educator about spinal cord injuries.

As with Christopher Reeve you can see that jealousy is one of the toughest feelings we come up against in our lives. There is not much worse than this aching sense that somehow life has been unfair to us, while amply rewarding someone else. It's even worse if that someone else is present in our daily lives, making it difficult for us to get the space we need to feel and heal our pain. We may be jealous of a sibling, a dear friend, or even famous personalities. We may even face the challenge of feeling jealous of our spouse, our child, or one of our parents. Whatever the case, we can normalize our experience by understanding that, as painful as it is, jealousy is a common human feeling.

Nevertheless, it is important that we not revel in our jealousy for too long, feeding it with inner talk or gossip with others. If we do, we run the risk of losing ourselves to its negative power. Jealousy has something good to offer us, though, and that is information about our own heart's desire. When we are jealous of certain people, we want what they have, and if we are to be conscious, we must acknowledge that. In this way, we discover what we want for ourselves, which is the first step to getting it. It may be a certain kind of relationship or a career. Whatever it is, it is possible that we could create it for ourselves, in our own lives, if we are able to honor our own desires.

Of course, there are times when we cannot heal our jealousy in this way, and then the lesson may be about acceptance and the understanding that our path is different from the paths of those around us. It may be hard to see now, but perhaps it will eventually be clear why our life has taken its particular path. In the end, the best cure for jealousy is the recognition that the life we have is full of its own meaning and beauty, utterly unique to us, a gift that could never be found in the life of another.

So you see how your mental outlook is a better, more effective way of achieving happiness than through external material sources or status. I know you want to have more and that's not bad as long as you understand what the real important things in life really are, which is..... (This is where you get to fill in what those things are for you). Let's hope that at least some of the important things in your life are peace, love and harmony.

Happiness vs. Pleasure

In reading the book "The Art of Happiness" by the Dalai Lama and Howard C. Cutler there is a chapter that talks about "happiness" vs. "pleasure." Now Wikipedia defines happiness as "a state of mind or feeling such as contentment, satisfaction, pleasure, or joy." A variety of philosophical, religious, psychological and biological approaches have been taken to defining happiness and identifying its sources.

Philosophers and religious thinkers have often defined happiness in terms of living a good life, or flourishing, rather than simply as an emotion. Happiness in this older sense was used to translate the Greek Eudaimonia, and is still used in virtue ethics. In everyday speech today, however, terms such as well-being or quality of life are usually used to signify the classical meaning, and happiness is reserved for the felt experience or experiences that philosophers historically called pleasure.

Pleasure is defined as "commonly conceptualized as a positive experience, happiness, entertainment, enjoyment, ecstasy, and euphoria." However, it is a difficult concept to define as the experience of pleasure differs from individual to individual.

People commonly experience this phenomenon through eating, exercise, sexuality, music, use of drugs, writing, accomplishment, recognition, service, indeed through any imaginable activity, even receiving pain (the medical term for deriving pleasure from receiving pain being masochism) and inflicting pain (sadism). It also refers to "enjoyment" related to certain physical, sensual, emotional or mental experiences.

Dr. Cutler mentions a situation, a discussion he had with a patient, during a therapy session. She was trying to figure out whether she should take a position in another town because she was so unhappy with the town she was living in, however she derived a great deal of pleasure in her present position. As she tried to weigh the differences, pros and cons, of moving or staying it became even more difficult because there were almost as many pros as there were cons. So the scale was pretty balanced.

Dr. Cutler then asks her whether she would derive greater pleasure or greater happiness in moving to this other town that she felt had a more ideal climate vs. the satisfaction she was getting from the job she was doing in the town where she presently lived?

She paused for a moment, uncertain what to make of the question. Finally she answered, "I don't know… You know, I think it would bring me more pleasure than happiness….Ultimately, I don't think I'd really be happy working with that clientele. I really do get a lot of satisfaction working with the kids at my present job."

She decided to remain in the town and not move because she would be happier doing what she was doing than changing to do something not as satisfactory because of a better climate.

As you can see from the definition of pleasure and happiness from Wikipedia and if you search both from a Thesaurus, you will find them to be synonyms. So are you here for pleasure or happiness? While you can derive pleasure from many things, good or bad for you, many of those things will not provide you with happiness.

Are you pleasured from sex? Are you pleasured from a massage? Are you pleasured from alcohol or drugs? Perhaps from some or all, I think you get the point. And, how about happiness? Will you be happy that you indulged in drinking, drugs or sex?

Happiness is something internal; it is a feeling that you get from doing good things and it is a feeling that you always want in your life. Happiness makes us more open, receptive, likeable and joyful. Pleasure is momentary, fleeting and doesn't always reside in good. Real happiness is achieved when doing pleasurable things that provide, happiness for others as well, not just fleeting moments of ecstasy.

So what is happiness for you? Know that it is a state of mind. Beyond the basic needs of food, clothing, shelter and love what else do you really need to be happy? Well, we could say that we want good health, a good-looking body, and a nice mate and family, however those things don't define happiness. Without anything else in your life you can still wake up every morning as happy and that will set the tone for the day.

Start Happy

For most of my life I never understood the concept. What do you mean just be happy? There is so much shit happening in my life there is no way I can be happy. Well, it took long enough but I finally got the concept. Just like the song, "Don't worry, be happy," we can all be happy.

Because I "got it," I now consciously wake up each morning with a good attitude. There are still things going on in my life that need addressing or taking care of or that I could see as a problem, but my being in a sour mood about these things won't make these problems any easier to deal with and they won't go away. I will not allow any of the "stuff" we all have to deal with each day put me in a bad mood and preclude my being happy even if some of the things I need to do I really don't want to do.

Are there things that come up during the day that could be upsetting and take you off course? Absolutely! But, you are in control; you have the ability to change a negative exterior happening, by not internalizing it, into a positive emotion.

Here's an example I know we can all relate to. I used to find driving to be a real challenge. Not that I can't drive, but it was hard for me to put my emotions aside when another driver did something I thought was inconsiderate, whether it affected me or someone else. These driving situations are one of my lessons in this life and I had to let it go. I cannot control what someone else is doing and my frustration and being upset at them only affects me. It has taken years to work through this, and I occasionally get a twinge, but when I do start to get upset I immediately have to laugh at myself and say "yes, I know this will keep happening to me until I just let it go and let it be.

"Whatever we plant in our subconscious mind and nourish with repetition and emotion will one day become a reality."

Earl Nightingale

Chapter Fifteen
Wisdom

It is said that wisdom is the quality or the state of being wise; having knowledge of what is true or right coupled with just judgment as to action; sagacity, discernment, or insight; scholarly knowledge or learning.

Wisdom is an ideal that has been celebrated since antiquity as the knowledge needed to live a good life. What this means exactly depends on the various wisdom schools and traditions claiming to help foster wisdom. In general, these schools have emphasized various combinations of the following: knowledge, understanding, experience, discretion, and intuitive understanding, along with a capacity to apply these qualities towards finding solutions to problems.

In many traditions, the terms wisdom and intelligence have somewhat overlapping meanings; in others they are arranged hierarchically, with intelligence being necessary but not sufficient for wisdom.

But has wisdom somehow been lost or forgotten or does it get confused with being wise? If you asked that question of a thousand people it is possible to get a thousand different answers. This same question was asked of some very notable people from all walks of life. Some were politicians, some actors and directors; others were scientists, mathematicians, clergy, musicians, and many notables who have made a name for themselves in society. None of them are necessarily wise or have they necessarily gained wisdom. Although I am not providing their complete statement here's the essence of what each said summarizing it in one word.

Wisdom is about: possibility, accepting, caring, changing, giving, doing, allowing, loving, experiencing, questioning, risking, decency, discovering, working, creating, learning, respecting, protecting, making a difference, and being the best.

141

Here we have twenty people, and twenty somewhat different answers. Is wisdom really that difficult to define or are we only able to define wisdom through the work that we do? Is it only luminaries, or well-known people or those who we believe have gained wisdom that can only define wisdom?

I think in general terms you could define wisdom as the ability to know the difference between understanding what you can change and what you cannot change and the ability to know the difference and accept either.

Does wisdom truly only come from knowledge and experience? Can you have wisdom at a young age, or does it only come with maturity? I'm not sure of that answer, however I do know that we all need to strive for having wisdom.

Do you know that there are classes you can enroll in where you can develop wisdom? I saw one class advertised as Wisdom 101, "A Course in Practical Wisdom." Is there such a thing as unpractical wisdom?

From my perspective wisdom is the sharing of experiences and knowledge, albeit a lot of it is common sense. The difference is how we apply this common sense. We all have the ability to keep going even when we face challenges in our lives, but basically it comes down to your attitude. We can have a positive attitude towards life, or a negative attitude. We can focus on the good or we can focus on the bad and keeping a positive mental attitude is one of the keys to success in having wisdom.

Wisdom does not just come from successful experiences for it is in our failures, where we usually learn the most. Or should I say experiences, because I have been told that there are no failures just an experience you don't want to duplicate. So even if we don't make always make wise decisions we can have gained wisdom.

How many positive experiences have you had that you remember vs. the negative experiences you had that you remember? Fortunately or unfortunately we seem to remember more of the negative experiences and more vividly. So again we see that wisdom is derived from making good and bad decisions or having good or bad experiences.

Well, here's where the rubber meets the road, so to speak. We can pretty much define wisdom and we know how you can achieve wisdom, but does that make you wise? Perhaps. Are they synonymous?

Wise, is a derivative of wisdom and is defined as; the ability to make sensible decisions and judgments on the basis of knowledge and experience; showing good sense or good judgment, capable of achieving some purpose or goal by cunning. Cunning almost sounds devious because it is defined as using wiliness or trickery. I would hope that we wouldn't use trickery in being wise.

While wise is similar to wisdom in its definition, being wise doesn't necessarily mean that you will have enough wisdom to make better decisions.

So, in essence you want to be both wise and have wisdom. Perhaps wise enough to understand that you need a lot of experience, or be able to use other people's experiences to gain wisdom. I asked this question on Facebook, "Is being wise and having wisdom the same thing?" Here are the replies I received.

"I think being wise is something you gain in time with your experiences and common sense and wisdom is the ability to use your experience and knowledge in order to make sensible decisions or judgments."

"They go together but having wisdom does not make you wise enough to apply it. Being educated does not make you smart. Etc."

"Being wise is something that comes with age and experience and you earn it. Having wisdom means you're having wisdom but not necessarily being wise."

"Being wise is putting the wisdom into action...meaning you know how to use this wisdom to make decisions."

"Wisdom is not on a book shelf to buy! If you gather all the books in the universe, one still may not be able to buy it. For it is something sacred and comes from within. Not every one is fortunate to have it. Being wise though, is something you can achieve by reading books or using someone's experience for that matter."

For example, you are wise to make a certain decision, but may not have the wisdom to see the consequences beyond! Wisdom is what prevents one to have the future negative consequences, so to speak. Not every wise decision is necessarily a good decision in the long run! It could be at that time, but not overall, only wisdom will determine that future assurance.

The overall problem is that most of us usually refuse to listen to words of wisdom and must experience life at any cost to gain wisdom. Words of wisdom many times come to us from the quotes of well-respected people who we believe have had such experiences from which they gained wisdom. Seems like if you have wisdom it can make your life easier and perhaps the lives of others easier that is if you are the leader of the group.

So will you rely on and use someone else's wisdom or will you wait to have the experience yourself? Of course then someone else's wisdom will be of no advantage to you. Let's hope that what you choose is a less bumpy road, filled with happiness, good health, a vibrant mind, as much wealth as you need and a spirit of giving.

Finally, I must add that I remember when wisdom came to us on a tiny piece of paper inside of a "Fortune Cookie." Now Fortune cookies usually only provide winning Lottery numbers perhaps we would be wise to play them, then again, perhaps not.

Chapter Sixteen
Wealth

Wikipedia says wealth is an abundance of valuable material possessions or resources. As well, "Wealth" refers to some accumulation of resources, whether abundant or not.

Most of us associate wealth with having money, our savings, our investments, our homes or other forms of "financial capital." But did you know that the word wealth comes from the Old English words "weal" (well-being) and "th" (condition) which taken together means "the condition of well-being."

I know that being wealthy in terms of having lot's of money is something that most of us want for it is a way to have financial security and comfortable surroundings. However, there are some that see wealth as unnecessary, a burden or a curse. It's not surprising that not everyone views wealth the same way, since all we seem to think about or talk about is the general economy or our personal finances.

So as you can see wealth in reality is about your well-being, whether it has to do with money, or your health, or your mind. Now you may still view wealth as financial resources or "money" and you may want a lot of money and you can have it, as long as you don't abuse it.

By abusing it I mean that money needs to be used for good and giving, hoarding it, as I will discuss later in the "Financial Wealth" section will not bring you more money although many believe it will. So first let's talk about wealth, as the condition of well-being, because well-being is about your overall wealth, which is really necessary for a complete and beautiful life. As James Arthur Ray puts it, it is your "Harmonic Wealth."

Harmonic Wealth is all about having harmony in every area of your life, which is being physically wealthy, mentally wealthy, financially wealthy, spirituality wealthy and relationally wealthy.

"There is nothing more marvelous than doing something you love to do and getting paid for it. It ceases to become work, money, and effort; and it becomes fun, your expression of the joy of life."

Stuart Wilde

In the following chapters I will be discussing well-being in all areas of our lives and I would like you to think about the meaning of wealth and well-being as synonymous. You will see that much of your success in having harmony in all areas has a lot to do with how you define your life as well as your definition of wealth and doing things that you love. Make your new definition of wealth clear and concise. Look at wealth as well-being because well-being is about having wealth in all five areas of your life. While having money is good it can't replace the well-being you want to experience with your relationships, or your physical health or with your spirituality. This means living your life with passion from your heart and not from your head.

I think and I hope that when your done with this book you will agree.

Chapter Seventeen
Physical Wealth

In being physically wealthy we are of course talking about our health. The meat suit you are wearing that covers the spiritual you, needs to be healthy to transport you around this orbiting globe. Sound weird? Just remember there are two of you, the physical you and the spiritual you. So since the only way to transport your spiritual you is through the physical you, during this lifetime, why not get around as ably as you can? What I'm talking about is with vitality, vigor and ease. Does this make sense?

While I can't speak for you I know that many people are uncomfortable with their physique, their overall health and physical ability. I know this because of all the studies and polls that have been taken. I know that approximately 70% of you are overweight, and 28% of you are obese, which means you're unfit and probably stressed out. So it really comes down to this. Do you really want to do something about your health and physique? Do you really want to stop spending money on doctors, unhealthy foods and diets that don't work? Do you want to stop spending 25 to 50% more on food than is required for good health? Do you think that getting fit is something someone else or some product will give you?

Now what I'm about to say has no judgments attached to it. I say it because I believe that it is important for you to take care of the whole you, not just some parts of you. So when I say it is important to be trim and eat right and do all those things that will assist you in living well, physically, it is without malice. I say it out of concern for you and not about judging you if you are not physically fit and in the 70% category.

Are some of us more challenged than others? Yes, of course, but this is no different from someone being challenged in other areas of their life. Some are challenged with getting finances under control, others with their relationships and still others with their spirituality or intellect. But right now we are going to address the physical aspects of your life.

Whether you have challenges in more than one area of your life or not you need to start somewhere, so why not take time to get back into life and start with the physical you. You can begin with the physical you right now just by paying a little attention to what you eat, how much you eat and with doing just a few minutes of exercise a day or a few times a week. Can you make 15 minutes available each day for exercise? Or how about one hour three times a week?

I have done a lot of research on being healthy and fit and I can tell you that you won't get healthy and fit by purchasing diet pills, diet programs or by just gobbling down handfuls of supplements. While supplements can assist you in getting the additional vitamins and minerals you need they alone are not the answers.

There are three basic things you must do to be healthy and fit. The first thing you need to work on is your mindset, which is by far the principal element to being healthy; the other elements are exercise and nutrition. Stop buying into diet fads, programs and more unless you are set on doing all the other things necessary for having a healthy life.

Conscious vs. Subconscious vs. Unconscious

While you have been told many times that fad diets don't work you still believe that the next one will be your salvation. It won't. Your feeling good and looking good starts with what's in your head. Just choosing good foods is not the complete answer and it's not just *what* you eat, but *how* you eat. You must pay attention to what you eat in choosing foods that are both nourishing and enjoyable that help support an overall healthy diet. Enjoying your food and relaxing as you eat are other key factors in being healthy.

While it's easy to follow these guidelines to find the foods that you like, which are good for you, it's your sub-conscious mind and it's deep-rooted messages that must change to overcome your being unhealthy and unfit. Of course if you're unconscious then you don't have worry about anything. Couldn't resist the joke.

The reason to start with your mind-set is because you must have the right outlook and really want to look and feel different. You must analyze the messages that you grew up with from your immediate family or friends, schoolmates or co-workers and how you think they saw you or see you. As well as how you see yourself today. Most of us see ourselves as imperfect, too tall, too short, too skinny, too fat, bulges here and there, too flabby, not enough muscle; and it can go on and on.

One of the first things you must deal with is your mindset by setting aside what others think and what you think they think about you and concentrate on what you really think about you. Right now if you are okay with yourself, regardless of your being overweight or underweight then there is no need to go further because there is no need to change you because of someone else's perception or the general populations view. However if you are unhappy with your health, body or level of fitness you need to recognize that and deal with it mentally first.

In the beginning it will take more will power than later on, as eating right and exercising become a regular routine. So let's start you off by answering these questions:

♥ How did I learn not to eat right?

♥ Why do I want to eat healthy?

♥ Am I willing to stick to a plan?

♥ Am I doing this for weight loss or to feel better or both?

♥ Who am I eating healthy for?

♥ Am I trying to impress someone else?

- ♥ What does feeling good mean to me?

- ♥ What does looking good mean to me?

- ♥ Is this just a fad or is it something I truly want the rest of my life?

The questions can be endless and they are trying to get at the core of your beliefs about you. Dieting is no different then trying to stop smoking. It's all about what you think regardless of what anyone else has to say.

Understand this, unless you are passionate about being healthy or loosing weight it will only last a short time. With anything you do for yourself if you aren't passionate about it you'll get frustrated, and/or depressed, blame the lack of results on someone or some program only to achieve the same lack luster results. You must do this for yourself. No one can tell you how you feel and how you look. If you look in the mirror and you're happy with how you look and you are happy with how you feel then you will have a better outlook on life and one less thing to get stressed about.

If you're not happy with your physicality and you really want to look and feel different, then you must ask yourself, are you up to the task of making that change? You can use the laws of intention and attraction, but remember it still takes action. You must see the new you in every minute of every day. It's like looking into a trick mirror, it's imagining and seeing yourself as how you will look tomorrow. While you may say this is how you want to be, it is seeing the new you now.

Here's the ploy, you have to see yourself in the future as if it were now, because you are creating the future and the past now. It's happening at this very minute. I can't stress this enough, your intention, what you are putting into the universe now will draw the energy necessary for you to be who you intend. Everything is happening now, the past and the future.

Right now is the time to decide who you are physically and how you will show up tomorrow. Will it be healthy, vibrant and alive, going and doing things you always wanted to do even when you're 90? Or will you continue to wish for a new you as if by magic the new you will appear? Most people can make it happen without surgery, without pills and without buying diet programs. So attract the information you need to eat healthy and if you can't join a gym start out at home or in your neighborhood in getting exercise. It is free.

Tassinello

Here are 14 Suggestions for getting healthy:

- Be sure you are changing your look for yourself and not someone else.

- Be aware that it takes time and it will not happen overnight.

- Take measurements now and once a week to see the results you may not physically see immediately.

- Do not weigh yourself everyday, only once a week and remember muscle is approximately 18% heavier than fat.

- Visualize your new body everyday.

- Set a workout routine that you can achieve and then increase it slowly.

- Allot enough time that is comfortable for you to make it happen and then increase it a little at a time.

- Make a list of the foods you like to eat and the foods that are good for you.

- Adjust portion sizes making sure you get enough calories and protein.

- Eliminate excessive alcoholic drinks.

- Always eat breakfast. It kick starts your metabolism to burn off more calories.

- Eat many smaller meals each day; it's better than 2 or 3 large meals. If you're going to eat a large meal make it lunch and not dinner.

- Cook at home. It' s cheaper and healthier. Stop eating fast food.

- Be patient. It takes time but with the right attitude and patience you will achieve the results you want.

Tassinello

Chapter Eighteen
Financial Wealth

Now I am not the guru of finances and this is not about where and how to invest. This is about your financial mindset. It's about how you think of your finances and how you think about your worth and your value.

Most of us are accustomed to looking at wealth strictly in financial terms of property and possessions. While wealth, as I spoke of earlier, is actually defined as well-being. Although there seems to be nothing in this life that is more sought after, or more debilitating (if you don't have it) and causes more relationship problems than money. Having the financial wealth you want does not have to be elusive. You can have exactly what you want.

Money is energy

To understand what money is and actually get a handle on its value is all in the way you view money. First, you must acknowledge that money is energy just like everything in this universe. How can you get to see and think about money as energy?

Let's first visualize it as electrons or atoms or molecules that happen to manifest themselves first as a tree and then processed into a piece of paper which is 2 ½" x 6", printed in green and black ink with numbers, words and symbols. What else is there that is printed and has value? Well, there are coupons, notes, IOUs, stocks, bonds and more. The only difference is that these other forms must be converted to the paper money to be used for everyday means of exchange. All financial instruments are just a medium of exchange no different than exchanging your time (your energy) for food or shelter or any other material item for another material item.

In reality money actually has no value, for if someone doesn't trade you something else for it, it has no value. It even says so on the dollar bill. Unlike some other forms of exchange, as was and still is done in some cultures by exchanging animals or vegetables, you can't eat it, or drink it, or drive it or live in it. I mean you really can't do anything else with it except trade it for something more tangible, unless you tape it together and build something with it.

Money, like everything, is energy, which is vibrating at a frequency of it's own, just like the energy of a car, a house, a boat, a tree, a mountain, the ocean and you. We're all energy vibrating at different frequencies. Yet we view money so differently, as if it were the Holy Grail. We do love the stuff, don't we? While it is okay to want money it is not okay to idolize it, or anything else for that matter and it is not okay to place it above everything else.

Money, that 2 ½" x 6" piece of paper energy is made from atoms just like you and me. Money is energy and you could think of it as such. You might visualize money like an electric current pulsing through wires. It is the energy that can help light up your life and the lives of others if properly used. Just like electric energy you cannot amass and hoard it as if you could not generate more of it. Money energy must be shared; it must be used to bring great projects into being; it must be used to provide for you, your family and others so everyone has enough and no one is lacking.

Money that green paper manufactured by the government will cease to exist at some time in the future. When that happens what will you do then? Before there were credit and debit cards money was the primary currency of exchange. But, today you are seeing less and less of it as we use plastic and the Internet for electronic transfers. So you may want to get used to not seeing that paper currency any longer and start now by recognizing it differently because you may never have another dollar or a coin in your purse.

When trading for goods and services becomes totally electronic the definition of money as green printed-paper will truly be an illusion and will in fact become energy. So what is money? It is energy and only a vehicle of exchange.

Your Real Wealth

Let's face it we all want money because it can make our lives a little easier and more comfortable. But you are not how much money you have or don't have. You are how you show up in this world. You are not just what you do, but how you do it. Real wealth is much more than property or possessions, and we know it intuitively, "real" or "genuine" wealth is you. It is your knowledge, skills, competencies, and other attributes that are you that will facilitate the creation of personal, social, and economic well-being. If you intend to have money you shall, just be sure to share it and use it for good.

While I want you to be aware of money as energy I also want you to look at all of the other material energy you have amassed and see if it's time to shed some of that wealth as well. Ask yourself, "How much of what I have do I really need?" "What purpose do these things serve in my life?" "Would some of these things be better used by someone else?" I'll bet you there are so many things on your shelves, in your closets, in your attic, basement or garage that you haven't seen in years, that you don't even know they exist. The universe is asking that you take that dormant energy and do something with it so it becomes useful once again, circulate that energy, someone else needs or wants it.

So here's what you can do. First maintain a mindset of being unattached to things, because you don't need these things, although you may want these things. While much of what you have may be something that gave you some satisfaction when you got it, it may be time to give it away. So much of what you have may have lost it's appeal, or luster or usefulness. You really don't need it you're just used to seeing it around. Clearing away things is good for your energy. So look closely at what you have and realize it is only a thing and that it may serve someone else better.

How to Re-energize Your Material Wealth

- Keep it because you really value and appreciate it and are using it.

- Sell it to someone who really wants it and who will use or appreciate it.

- Give it away to someone who needs and wants it.

- Make an effort to have it properly recycled and a s a last resort send it to the trash.

Any of these options will bring more light and energy into your life and the lives of others.

Chapter Nineteen
Relational Wealth

We all know what a relationship is, don't we? Sounds like a silly question doesn't it? Perhaps it's not a silly as it sounds. As you might have guessed I like to begin with a definition so we are all on the same page.

An *inter*personal relationship is a relatively long-term association between two or more people. This association may be based on emotions like love and liking, regular business interactions, or some other type of social commitment. Interpersonal relationships take place in a great variety of contexts, such as between family or friends, a marriage, acquaintances, at work, clubs, neighborhoods, or in churches. They may be regulated by law, custom, or mutual agreement, and are the basis of social groups and society as a whole.

An intimate relationship is a particularly close interpersonal relationship. It is a relationship in which the participants know or trust one another very well or are confidants of one another, or a relationship in which there is physical or emotional intimacy. Finally there is the relationship with you.

So which of these relationships is the most important? While we all may have our own interpretation, the most important relationship you want to understand and to develop is your relationship with yourself. May sound silly, but it's the one that has the biggest impact on your life.

Well you may as well ask, why is that? Let's face it if you can't have a good relationship with yourself, how can you have a good relationship with anyone else? As Marcus Aurelius once said:

"He who lives in harmony with himself lives in harmony with the universe."

Marcus Aurelius has a great point. You must be happy within yourself to begin to live in harmony with others. Do little things annoy you? Do you typically feel like people are constantly criticizing you? Do you wake up cranky carrying over the previous days problems and don't even want to get out of bed? Of course this list can go on and on and I'm not here as your therapist. However, if situations like this are constant in your life then you obviously don't have a good relationship with yourself. If you're unhappy, it shows and it affects everyone around you.

Assessing You

So how do you see yourself? How do you feel about yourself? Do you like who you are? Do you like who you are around others? What are the qualities you see in yourself that you like and what are the things about you that you don't like? If you have a difficult time being alone then how can you expect anyone else to want to be with you, and why would you want to have that kind of relationship?

If you were looking at yourself and interacting with yourself on any level and in any relationship what would you say about yourself? And since only you are answering these questions and no one else is going to hear them or judge them, it's time to be very honest with yourself. Remember ego will deceive you, so be very clear about how you act and what you do.

It is amazing how we can delude ourselves into believing we are someone we are not. For instance how many times do you think you are truly funny without the biting sarcasm; you know the sarcasm that cuts like a knife. How loving are you? I mean the love that truly comes from the heart where there is nothing in it for you, except to know that you helped someone in some way without any expectation. How big is that? Most of your time is spent with someone close to you, personally or in business, isn't it? Do you really want those relationships to be difficult? I think not, yet most times the only charity we give is to someone we don't know believing that we are charitable. You probably remember this saying "Charity begins at home," and that doesn't just mean giving money to a family member.

Instinctively you really know this, and in reality you shouldn't need to be taught this, but here we are learning about it. This is all about your EGO-your EGO, the part of you that does those deceitful things. It wants you to believe that you have done something so wonderful for someone else when in reality you did it to get something in return. Don't be too hard on yourself; sometimes it takes someone else to point this out, to give you a nudge to move in a new direction, to have you remember what you do and how you can be better.

Until you love yourself and act without expectation of getting something in return your relationships are incomplete. In forming a perfect relationship with yourself take inventory of all of your wonderful qualities and accomplishments. Something I mentioned earlier is that we have a tendency to dwell on the negative things in life. They seem to be more prevalent than the positive things we experience, and that's why it is so important to take stock of your attributes. You need to see all the good and great things about yourself and fall in love with yourself. This is not to be conceited or selfish, but an act of self-love. You know there is so much to love about yourself. Don't let the past get in the way of a new and beautiful today.

Here's a true story. I knew this girl who was very strong willed and determined. At sixteen she became pregnant. While her parents wanted her to either have an abortion or give the child away she decided that she would have the child and be a mom. Now she was lucky that her boyfriend stuck by her and they got married. While they had a tough relationship she made the effort to raise her children well. She did almost anything necessary for the love and care of herself and her children. Think about what she had to go through at such a young age to become a successful woman. Now I tell you this because she doesn't acknowledge all the good and great things about herself because her parents were disappointed in her for not following their wishes and doing what they thought was best. Imagine thinking that you failed somehow because of someone else's thoughts about you.

So look closely at all the great things you have done and acknowledge yourself for them. You know who you are and you are not what you think others think of you. I'm sure you've done a lot more than you take credit for.

"Know thyself and you will possess the keys to the universe and the secrets of the gods"

The Oracle of Delphi

So why not begin by listing all of those attributes now. When you're done you may continue reading. I'm being a bit facetious here, however it is usually good to do things as they come along, otherwise we tend to put things aside and not get to it. Or you can just bookmark this page and make that list later. Probably better now, don't you think?

Relationships With Others

Now it's time to talk about relationships with others. I'm not going to get into specifics of how men act or how women act or how to handle specific relationships. There are plenty of so-called relationship self-help websites with people claiming to know what you need to do and what you shouldn't do. I can only tell you that everything I am talking about is to have you understand that it is you, who are the key to this puzzle and making things work. It is you who are in control and it is you who must be the change. Gandhi was so correct when he said,

"You must be the change you want to see in this world."

You cannot change or mold someone into being who you think they should be because of how you think they should be or act. There is one more quote to consider, which is from Ben Franklin,

"A man convinced against his will is of the same opinion still."

You can only change yourself and you cannot force change upon anyone else, they must come to that change on his or her own.

Of course your relationship with others is very complex. There is no one formula, method or technique that can solve all of your relationship problems. However there are general guidelines that can be useful. The most crucial is the thought of compassion.

The Dalai Lama put it this way. "A simple prescription of, it's very important to be compassionate; you must have more love isn't enough. One effective means of teaching someone how to be more warm and compassionate is to begin by using reasoning to educate the individual about the value and practical benefits of compassion, and also have them reflect on how they feel when someone is kind to them. In a sense this primes them, so there will be more of an effect as they proceed in their efforts to be more compassionate."

While the Dalai Lama is using a method to try and show someone how it feels if someone is not compassionate with you, you must feel compassion not just recognize it. It is that component of love for another, which allows you to understand someone else's pain, and desires to help them.

"Compassion is that which makes the heart of the good move at the pain of others. It crushes and destroys the pain of others."

The Buddha

Compassion is a profound human emotion prompted by the pain of others. It is more vigorous than empathy, as the feeling commonly gives rise to an active desire to alleviate another's suffering. While empathy is equally as important as compassion, empathy is the capability to share and understand another's emotion and feelings. It is often characterized as the ability to "put oneself into another's shoes," or in some way experience what the other person is feeling.

Both compassion and empathy are important. Empathy allows oneself to figuratively put themselves in another's shoes to see how they would react to the situation. What you want to do is stop thinking about your viewpoint and actually visualize from the perspective of the other person. You don't have to agree, but you must see from the other side, thus reducing conflicts and problems.

Through relationships we learn about ourselves, because people around us reflect back to us who we are. This is why so many relationships are difficult. If your relationships cause you to struggle, ask yourself, "Why are my relationships so hard?" What is your relationship about that prevents it from going your way? What is your level of giving and receiving? Are you allowing yourself to be unhappy, and if you are, why? Don't you want to change that?

Have you ever done this? You dated someone's brother or the sister just to be close that person, the one you actually love? How many times have you done things you really don't want to just because you believe the outcome will change? You have a right to be happy, but sometimes compromising for your happiness also compromises someone else's happiness. In not being true to yourself you are also being untrue to another.

If your psychological state causes you suffering, it will either be a by-product of your physical state or of your attitude. Which one applies to you?

In summation, spend time with yourself, either in meditation or at minimum without any distractions and get to know yourself. Then look at all of your relationships and know that the one common denominator of these relationships is you. So whatever issues there are with one, some or all; you must look at yourself and consider changing your perception and/or changing how you act.

While change isn't always easy and seeing the real you can be even more difficult, take the time to meditate and do some soul searching. Recognize that life is about compassion, sharing, allowing and not re-acting. It really allows you to become more peaceful and grateful for everything you have. As you become more thoughtful about what you do and how you act you see the changes in yourself and everyone around you.

Right now you can begin creating your perfect life, knowing that there are always lessons to be learned. Remember, it doesn't happen overnight, although done with conviction and commitment you will see results very quickly.

Want to see a change in your relationships? Then be the change because it all starts with you.

As they say "Life is what you make it." Put a smile on your face, change your perspective and use positive language in what you say and do.

Tassinello

Easy tips for beginning each day

1. Wake up with a smile. All you have to do is laugh at yourself while still in bed and I guarantee you will smile.

2. Change your routine. Get out of bed like you're on vacation and get going for some fun.

3. Greet the world and your family with a "good morning" and a smile.

4. Visualize your whole day going the way you want (do not think about any potential problems).

5. Start by doing something you like, perhaps a short meditation or put on some lively music.

6. Have a nice healthy breakfast, sitting down. Don't rush it.

7. Change how you interact with family, friends, and coworkers.

8. Just observe what happens around you and your interaction with others and don't judge.

9. Go with the flow. Although you have intentions and expectations for how the day should go, allow the day to unfold and don't get upset with the changes. Be like the sea and ebb and flow with the day.

10. At the end of the day reflect on the days happenings and learn from all that transpired. Look at how things were different from usual and how your changing changed people and circumstances.

11. Do it again tomorrow.

Tassinello

Chapter Twenty
Intellectual Wealth

Intelligence (also called intellect) is an umbrella term used to describe a property of the mind that encompasses many related abilities, such as the capacities to reason, to plan, to solve problems, to think abstractly, to comprehend ideas, to use language, and to learn.

Obviously individuals differ from one another in their ability to understand complex ideas, to adapt effectively to the environment, to learn from experience, to engage in various forms of reasoning, to overcome obstacles by taking thought. Although these individual differences can be substantial, they are never entirely consistent. A person's intellectual performance will vary on different occasions, in different domains, and as judged by different criteria.

Concepts of "intelligence" are attempts to clarify and organize this complex set of phenomena. Although considerable clarity has been achieved in some areas, no such conceptualization has yet answered all the important questions and none commands universal assent. Indeed, when two-dozen prominent theorists were recently asked to define intelligence, they gave two-dozen somewhat different definitions.

Suffice it to say how you define intelligence matters not. It is what you do with your intelligence and how you continue to improve your intelligence. Intellectual wealth (well-being) can only be achieved through continued learning. So how are you using your mind? Are you spending most of your time in a vegetative state by watching TV and tuning out, or are you feeding your mind with stimulating and thought provoking material?

Statistics say that the average person watches TV about 25hrs a week. That translates into about 10 years of TV watching by the time we reach the age of 70. While many people say that any amount of TV watching is bad, others will say that there are some very interesting and informative programs on TV that are educational and helpful.

Of course where you fall into this fray is an individual perspective. Let's just say that too much mindless, non-thought provoking TV doesn't make a lot of sense. You need to exercise your brain as you would your physical body. Or it, like your body, will wither away and die. Besides the "neurobic" exercises suggested below getting out and playing a sport or any other type of physical exercise also exercises the brain.

Here's what Laurie Pawlik-Kienlen has to say about ways to develop your mind.

"Ten Ways to Improve Your Brain Health."

1. Do "neurobic" exercises. Certain cognitive exercises can create new associations between different brain parts, says neurobiologist Lawrence Katz of Duke University. Neurobics include getting dressed or showering in the dark, switching what you normally wear on one side to the other (e.g., put your watch or bracelet on your opposite wrist), using your opposite hand to brush your teeth, hanging pictures upside down, and cooking ethnic foods that you've never prepared before.

2. Limit your alcohol intake. The more alcohol you consume, the lower your brain volume becomes. Scientists at Wellesley College in Massachusetts found that low to moderate levels of alcohol help protect your health from cardiovascular disease, but heavy drinking shrinks brains. These researchers define heavy drinking as more than 14 drinks per week, moderate drinking as 8 to 14 drinks per week, and low as less than 7 drinks per week. To increase your intellect and cognitive ability, keep the alcohol consumption to a minimum.

3. Try something new. An active brain can slow the mental decline that comes with age. "A lifetime of good mental habits pays off," says University of Alberta researcher Dr. Dennis Foth. "People who are curious at a young age are more likely to be mentally active and stay active as they age. And we found it's never too late to start. With a little effort, even people in their 70s and 80s can see dramatic improvements." Memorizing poetry, learning a new musical instrument, or taking Spanish, French or other language lessons are great ways to strengthen your memory and improve your brain health.

4. Smell the sandalwood. "Natural scents have a direct pathway to the brain and research shows that some chemical constituents of aromatherapy oils, particularly sesquiterpenes can cross the blood-brain barrier and increase oxygen flow to the brain," says Michelle Schoffro Cook, doctor of natural medicine and author of The Brain Wash. Extra oxygen increases energy, immune function, positive moods, and learning. Frankincense and sandalwood are particularly effective at increasing oxygen levels in the brain. An easy way to improve your brain health could involve a little aromatherapy.

5. Do the tango. Dance requires twists and turns that strengthen brain connections. Learning the cha-cha-cha can nourish brain cells, which translates to quick thinking in the real world. "Exercise can protect the brain against environmental toxins by counteracting free radicals and reducing inflammation," says Schoffro Cook, author of The Brain Wash. Physical activity is one of the best ways to promote the growth of new brain cells and strengthen your memory.

6. Sleep well. Your brain requires huge amounts of energy to function properly; sleep boosts memory and allows your brain to process information. "Though it's not sexy, the traditional sleep advice is still effective," says Dr Rachel Morehouse of the Atlantic Sleep Centre. Sleep little – if at all – during the day because naps rob you of sleep at night. To improve your brain health, get up and go to bed at set times. Stay active but avoid exercising in the evening because it keeps you awake. Wind down before you go to bed with music or a book. Enjoy healthy food, eat light meals at night, and avoid caffeine.

7. Volunteer. "Good Samaritans have been found to have lower stress levels and a sense of well-being, factors that add up to better overall health, including brain health," says Schoffro Cook, author of The Brain Wash. The brain benefits of volunteering include increased mental functioning and better communication skills. The key may be in the "helper's high" – the sense of calmness and well-being that comes from helping others. Volunteering can also improve your brain health by raising your self-esteem and feelings of self-efficacy.

8. Socialize with people. Talking can improve memory and thinking skills, says Oscar Ybarra, a psychologist at the University of Michigan. Further, he believes that visiting with a friend or neighbor may be as helpful as doing a crossword puzzle. About his study, he said, "Short-term social interaction lasting for just 10 minutes boosted participants' intellectual performance as much as engaging in so-called "intellectual" activities for the same amount of time."

9. Strive for variety. Don't rely on a particular practice, supplement, or food to improve your brain health. Instead, incorporate different activities into your life. For instance, take a child hiking if you normally spend time with adults; go for a run instead of the usual yoga class. The more you challenge your brain and body, the healthier and stronger they become.

10. Reduce your exposure to neurotoxins. Harmful chemicals, food additives, and chemically altered ingredients can harm your brain and body health. While it's not possible to completely eliminate pollution from your environment, you can limit it. Pure products, organic produce, natural fragrances, whole foods, and fresh air will improve your brain health and strengthen your memory.

These are just a few ways to exercise your brain and increase your intellectual capacity. Almost anything you participate in takes brainpower and thus exercises the mind. Conversely and unfortunately, most TV and movie watching is of little intellectual benefit and mostly an escape from reality.

So if you really want to understand yourself and others, manifest a great life and increase your financial wealth you must exercise your brain by solving problems, having conversations, reading or writing, or doing anything worthwhile.

Tassinello

Chapter Twenty-One
Spiritual Wealth

Spiritual wealth comes from your one-on-one relationship with your source. Earlier I defined spiritual as not being affiliated with a religion. Meaning it is not Jewish, Catholic, Baptist, Protestant, Greek Orthodox, Buddhist, Muslim, Hindu or any other of the hundreds of religions man has created. While spiritualism is not attached to any religion it does not mean you cannot have a religious affiliation to be spiritual. I have no judgments about how you practice to speak with God, but there is only one Light whatever you choose to call him, her or it and it is not biased or judgmental.

As Jalal ad-Din Muhammad Rumi the Persian poet and theologian from 1207 to 1273 ad said:

"If you think there is an important difference between being a Jew, or a Christian, or a Buddhist, or a Muslim, or a Hindu, then you are making a decision between your heart, what you love with, and the way you act in the world."

I know that many of you who are reading this understand that you are a spiritual being having a physical experience; you are hard-wired to have a spiritual component in your life and that you want desperately to figure out who you are, why you are here and what to do to have everything you so deserve and be at peace with the world.

Your mission is to realize your full potential, gain peace and harmony and live a happy and prosperous life. It is to join with your neighbors, all the people of the world, to enhance your minds and souls, to give and to receive all that God has provided. "To tear down the walls of the prison we have created and live in the Light." As Michael Berg states, it is to "Become Like God" not be God.

I will share with you parts of a chapter from Michael Berg's book "Becoming Like God." As Michael states, "We are in a ceaseless battle against the negative force that operates within our skin, inside our brain, inside our cells, which relegates us to a robotic existence, and then kills us as a reward."

The opponent is our ego. Every moment we have a choice of how to operate and just like a computer; we have an opportunity to upgrade our operating system.

What Michael has written about and what this book is about is in providing you with information and an arsenal of tools for living a better life.

First, we must recognize that we are in a prison and not a luxury hotel. I'm speaking metaphorically about your soul and not your surroundings.

Second, there is the power in you to act and begin to refuse to accept death and suffering as your final reality.

Third, is you must have ultimate clarity and focus on the goal and the means of breaking down the prison walls to become like God.

Fourth, you need to recognize and unmask your opponent, because he will trick, confuse and deceive you at every turn.

Fifth, you must have certainty of your extraordinary potential to become like God for our goal to be achieved.

Sixth, is being ever vigilant against comfort. You must gladly plunge into the realm of discomfort to begin the destruction of the ego and transformative sharing.

Seventh, are your ceaseless efforts, focus and remembrance of the ultimate goal, and refusal to settle for anything less than total transformation.

Will your journey be difficult? Yes, and for some more difficult than others yet so very rewarding to be able to finally live without the confines of the prison you have created. Imagine being free, to roam and enjoy the beauty of life without restriction. It is interesting how you know how to fight for a mate or a job or for your country's so-called rights and freedoms, but you don't put up a fight for your own salvation and spiritual freedom.

Every one of us has a window in our hearts, a window that shows us what we could be. Our job, whenever we come across somebody in pain, is to take him or her to that window and point out what is waiting for him or her on the other side of suffering. As Stuart Wilde titled his book, "Life Was Never Meant to Be a Struggle."

Your ultimate job is to help the world achieve a critical mass of people on the path to becoming like God, so that pain and suffering, and death will vanish. While the opponent will try to make you forget, you will not. While he will try to weaken your resolve, you will not let this happen. You will create the crack in you prison wall and find the doorway out and remove your pain and suffering and live in the Light. Your destiny is to become <u>like</u> God.

"Love, compassion and kindness are the anchors of life"

It is by your commitment and ultimate desire, which will allow you to transcend the everyday difficulties you perceive because it is all a deception. This deception is a perception you have that you believe is real and you make real by buying into the drama. You have the ability to rise above all of the drama, pain, discomfort, angst, irritation, dilemmas, problems, frustration, aggravation and any other negative thing that is happening. It is in your willpower that you can overcome anything and everything by your choosing. You are in control and you are in command. So be responsible and use your ability to achieve all that you wish to achieve.

God and enlightenment is not about what religion you practice, but how you practice everyday to bring peace, love and compassion to yourself and the world. Even though there seems to be no easy way, and your path is not paved like a newly laid concrete walkway you will get there. You will have to navigate this path over rocks, boulders, and trees, across waterways and more. It will take will power, but your thoughts, words and actions will let you overcome whatever difficulties you perceive and you will find many others to support you along this road to happiness and contentment.

The Ten (10) Spiritual Keys

Here are "Ten Keys" for you to manifest an incredible life and to help your neighbor do the same. Please be forewarned that these are merely tools designed to help you connect to energy. You are free to use some, all or none of these as you dictate and follow your path. I say this because you must use these keys and this information correctly for you. Meaning it must be with an open heart and a true desire to give and receive with compassion and love. It is up to you. Remember love is the key to well-being; and your knowledge is the power to a beautiful life; use it wisely.

1.   **Practice Gratitude:** Live each day with gratitude and be thankful for everything you have in your life. Also be thankful for what you are manifesting today. Remember everything is happening in the present, not in the future.

2.   **Affirm and Visualize:** Write down who you are and who you want to be as if you were that right now by visualizing yourself, being whoever you are. Feel it, smell it, and taste it as if it were happening right now, even your interactions with others.

3.   **Forgiveness:** Let it go, let it be and let God. You must forgive others and yourself. Getting angry and holding on to anger creates acid in your body, which affects your health, your mood and your ability to think rationally. Acknowledge what happened and understand the message and the lesson.

4.   **Meditate:** This is a great way to get centered, to relax, and allow all thoughts to flow through you giving them no value. It puts you in alignment and connects you to your higher self. As you leave your meditative state you can then visualize and clarify what you want, which you are and how to accomplish your goals.

5.   **Messages:** Learn how to recognize them by exploring your subconscious and conscious mind. Remember dreams and write them down in the middle of the night if you are awakened. There are messages, signs and

symbols all around you, all the time, helping you to move toward enlightenment. Pay attention to those messages even if it is via a confrontation, and please don't shoot the messenger, bless them.

6.   **Judgment:** It's time to stop judging others as well as yourself. Judging stops you from listening, hearing or seeing the message. Be an observer by just acknowledging the differences and accepting whoever they are. You can learn so much from the most unlikely people. Don't get too attached to your specific desires as you never know when they may turn into something even better than you wanted because you left the door to opportunity open.

7.   **Energy Waves:** Energy just like waves in an ocean is continually moving, flowing and cycling. Continue to move your energy, which are your spirit, your money and your time by giving it on a regular basis. Anytime you or your resources are stagnant it stops the flow. You must give to receive.

8.   **Control:** Remain diligent to your ego's devious methods of trickery. Resist negativity, as all negative thoughts come from the adversary, all of them. Don't let the opponent have you lead a mediocre life. Everyone alive has a destiny to fulfill and infinitely richer than you may know at this moment. Live into your potential.

9.   **Remain in the Light:** Stop selfish actions. Whether it is philandering, lying, or fighting with someone over a parking spot, all selfish actions are subject to the law of Cause and Effect. So every negative action causes a negative reaction somewhere down the line.

10.   **Think Immortality:** While this may sound crazy it is possible. Everything is made up of atoms and atoms never die so why do we? As difficult as this is to comprehend it can be achieved. I want you to visualize atoms as if they are puzzle pieces or Legos. Okay, now when the puzzle pieces fit together it forms a picture and with Legos you make things like, a robot, a fort, a car or whatever. When you disassemble what you made the puzzle pieces and Legos still exist, don't they? It's the same with atoms. Atoms make up everything in

existence and they never die. So is it possible for you to keep your atoms linked together to keep you alive forever? It is possible so why not at least think immortality and treat your atoms well so they stay linked together? Treating them well physically and also spiritually by loving you. If you truly Love yourself you will take care of yourself. Physically you will eat better and exercise and spiritually you will practice all the things I mentioned in keys 1 through 9.

Tassinello

Summary

The information and tools are here, and you've been given the information but only through doing them without hesitations will you achieve your dreams.

Do not be ashamed of who you are or what and how you practice your faith and do not condemn others for what and how they practice. Life is meant for everyone to enjoy, not just a few.

"Gentlemen, my honor lies in no-one's hand but my own, and it is not something that others can lavish on me; my honor, which I carry in my heart, suffices me entirely, and no one is judge of it and able to decide whether I have it." - Otto von Bismark

Here is your daily exercise. With time you will know it instinctively and you will wonder why you did not do this everyday before. Only know this, be grateful that you have recognized it now and that the rest of your life will be better in every respect.

Practice tolerance every moment.

Practice love every moment.

Practice truth every moment.

Practice giving every moment.

Practice allowing every moment.

Practice compassion every moment.

Practice empathy every moment.

Practice peace every moment.

Practice fairness every moment.

Practice integrity every moment.

Practice respect every moment.

Practice honor every moment.

Don't turn away and don't give up; you need to do this for yourself and for the world. We are all depending on you to do this, for us to do this. As you apply all of these traits of yourself so you in return will receive them.

"Live your life from inspiration, not obligation or desperation."

Fortunately, I know your determination is strong and you have what it takes to establish new goals and to reach them according to your schedule. Don't succumb to any fears of inadequacy, for they are probably based on some prior failure rather than what's happening in the present.

"The true perfection of man lies not in what man has, but in what man is." - Oscar Wilde

Believe it or not, your faith can move mountains. Through God's power within you, anything is possible. While you may still think you are your body, in actuality, you are a mountain-moving machine.

It's Your Life - Reclaim It, Transform It and Make It Everything You've Ever Wanted It to Be!

My hope is that I have helped create awareness for you where you may have been lacking and have provided you with another perspective and as well furnished you with some guidance. Like you, I am another of God's instruments. Through my writing this book has come into existence bringing you information for our awakening and victory. If not me, then who? Perhaps it is you.

With Light and Love,

Arthur James Tassinello

References

The following resources were used in my research and as material for this book.

Ashlag, Rav Yehuda – *The Zohar*, The Kabbalah Centre International, Inc., 2003

Berg, Michael – *Becoming Like God*, Kabbalah Centre International, 2004

Berg, Rav P.S. – *Kabbalistic Astrology*, Kabbalah Centre International, 2000

Berg, Yehuda – *True Prosperity*, Kabbalah Centre International, 2005

Berg, Yehuda – *Beyond Blame*, Kabbalah Centre International, 2006

Campbell, Joseph – *The Inner Reaches of Outer Space*, St. James Press, 1985

Dyer, Dr. Wayne W. – *The Power of Intention*, Hay House, Inc., 2004

Hanh, Thich Nhat – *Peace is Every Step*, Bantum Books, 1991

Hawkings, Stephen – *The Illustrated A Brief History of Time*, Bantum Dell, 1996

Hawkings, Stephen – *The Universe in a Nutshell*, Bantum Dell, 2001

Hicks, Jerry and Ester – *The Law of Attraction*, Hay House, Inc., 2006

Lama, Dalai – *The Art of Happiness*, by Howard C. Cutler, M.D., Riverhead Books, 1998

Ray, James Arthur w/Linda Sivertsen – *Harmonic Wealth*, Hyperion, 2008

Ryan, M.J – *The Power of Patience*, Broadway Books, 2003

Walsch, Neale Donald – *Conversations with God*, Putnam, 1995

Wilde, Stuart – *Life Was Never Meant to Be a Struggle*, Hay House, Inc., 1987

One final note about these authors is that I encourage you to read their books or subscribe to their emails as well. Perhaps what they have written or the words they use will resonate within you, and you will receive the message(s) you were meant to receive. As they say, **"When the student is ready, the teacher will come."**